THE PROBLEMS OF INDIAN YOUTH

THE PROBLEMS OF INDIAN YOUTH

DHURJATI PRASAD MUKERJI

GYAN

Published by

Gyan Publishing House
5, Ansari Road
Daryaganj, New Delhi-110002
Phone: 011-47034999, 9811692060
E-mail: books@gyanbooks.com

Distribution Network
gyanbooks.com
India, USA, Canada, UK, Australia

ISBN: 978-93-7169-218-2 (PB)

First Published, 1946

2nd Impression 2026

Printed at: Gyan Press, Delhi.

THE PROBLEMS OF INDIAN YOUTH
Author: DHURJATI PRASAD MUKERJI

THE PROBLEMS OF INDIAN YOUTH

BY

Dhurjati Prasad Mukerji

LUCKNOW UNIVERSITY

HIND KITABS

PUBLISHERS : BOMBAY

TO

KUMAR

AND

HIS FRIENDS

PREFACE

I have had more pleasure in building up this book than any other. First, the drudgery of writing, and re-writing, checking and revision I did not have to undergo, because my addresses and talks, which form the chapters here, were either dictated when they were to be read out, or taken down in shorthand by one or two devoted pupils in the course of impromptu delivery. Beyond slight amendments here and there, the text remains of the spoken word. I am sincerely grateful to those who made things easy for me. My special obligations are to the *Student* and the *Social Welfare* in which a good bit of the text appeared.

Secondly, these pages are charged with happy memories. In fact, they are the happiest that I can muster. They conjure up bright faces, keen eyes, high heads and broad hearts of boys and girls in their teens. Modern Indian Society, in a sense, does not recognize Youth. In this ancient land, there are only two seasons, summer and winter, with no vernal interlude, no maturity of autumn. And yet, I have seen the touch of spring in the sudden awakening of a mind by an idea and an ideal. Even these years, 1939-1945, with their unbeatable record of intellectual suppression, emotional frustration and a systematic breaking of the will could not blight it out of existence. I wonder if it will ever be realized how the Youth—and may I add, those who loved them, suffered. The generation that passed out of the University between 1939 and 1945 could not bloom. But the sap did not dry up. I used to sense it during my addresses. It made me hope and live, in spite of my grief at the macabrous situation in the country. My speeches carried both the feelings. If they bore one more than another, the audience generously understood the reason They put it to my age in which idealism generally defends itself by cynicism.

One thing in particular used to disturb me, and it was the rift in the ranks of the student community. All 'parties' would come to me. Individually, their conduct was irreproachable. There was not a single member of the Indian Students' Federation—and I know most of the lot—who in thought or deed could stab the country in the back. All of them led exemplary lives. They were serious-minded and disciplined. A meeting of 12,000 people was managed by them with the smoothness of a Duke's household. They did wonders in relieving distress; they wanted the Hindus and the Muslims to come together; they appreciated the menace of Fascism. They did nothing in the nature of a national wrong or a social sin. My idea was that they overdid everything. Their slogan was ill-advised; their emphasis was not correct; they misunderstood the national sentiment. But then, the right to commit mistakes is the divine right of Youth. One does not expect Youth to behave like Plato's elders whose philosophic right is confined to correction.

On the other hand, those who plunged into the struggle of 1942, or were clapped into prison for unknown reasons, were the very salt of India. To call them Fifth Columnists was a libel, a calumny. I know them, and some of them inside out. They would have been in the front line against the Japs if they came. They suffered, because they loved India. And what that suffering was I know. If their spirit was not unconquerable, they would have betrayed. That they did not, not a single son of a woman among them. And yet, my impression was that they believed in the spontaneity of revolutionary processes It made them lean heavily on fervour. But then such a faith was Bakunin's, and even Rosa Luxemburg's. Our revolutionary leaders were then inside the Jail. No authoritative instructions had been left. What came instead often confused more than they clarified Compliments are being showered on these brave young people. They deserve it more than people know. All are naturally proud of them; but can they be proud of serving those who did not instruct them in the technique of this grim business of modern rebellions. So, if the Youth failed as rebels, it was certainly not their fault. They have succeeded in teaching themselves. That is probably the best education,' if only the costs were less.

Anyhow, all that conflict of ideologies—that silly word—is silenced for the time being. How long one never can tell. I have no desire to take it up. My analysis is that our young people quarrelled because they did not get a chance of showing their full potentialities. It is the same with the Hindu-Muslim question. Somewhere there resides an urge for creation which, if baulked, leads to all manner of squabbles. It is something more than an instinct, more than the elan vital of Bergson or the Life Force of Bernard Shaw. Indian Philosophy understands it as a unifying agency. Well, I am not sure. Still, there may be something in it, provided it is not confined to the individual being. Probably, India's Youth will give the correct answer in the near future, when India enters the self-chosen phase of her history.

18th November 1945 D. P. M.

CONTENTS

		PAGE
I	INDIAN YOUTH IN CRISIS	... 1
II	SOCIOLOGY OF THE INDIAN YOUTH	... 17
III	INDIAN YOUTH: THE MARGINAL BEING	... 29
IV	INDIAN YOUTH IN URBAN SETTING	... 40
V	THE INDIAN YOUTH AS WARDS OF GUARDIANS	... 48
VI	THE TEACHER-STUDENT NEXUS	... 65
VII	WHAT TO READ—A FEW PRINCIPLES OF SELECTION	... 78

1. INDIAN YOUTH IN CRISIS[1]

Friends,

I thank you sincerely for the signal honour you have conferred on me by asking me to preside over the eighth session of the All-India Students' Conference. When I remember the names of your previous presidents I am overwhelmed by the sense of my incompetence. They form an illustrious list of men whose gifts of leadership trained in the field of action and whose sacrifice in the wake of their ideals would make any country proud of them. It was not a wise decision on your part to have added my name to that glorious roll. My responsibility is increased a thousand-fold when I realize that this session of your Conference is not only meeting after a number of years, but it is meeting at a period which I consider to be the most critical period in India's history.

If ever there was a crisis facing our future, it is now. A pall of frustration hangs over India. If we leave aside those who are battening on our misfortunes, the profiteers and their parasites, there is hardly any section of our people that does not feel unhappy at the turn events are taking. Famine is not yet over and its aftermath— probably worse in its long-term effects upon the next generation—is very much with us. Gandhi-Jinnah talks failed, and after the failure, the two communities are drifting apart. Bitterness is in every speech; it colours almost every social sentiment; the students are fighting between themselves; hatred stalks the land whose genius has been a loving assimilation of the opposite and the disparate; culture is at a standstill. Friends, I

1 Presidential Address at the eighth session of the All-India Students' Conference.

wonder if I were the right person to take you out of the slough of despond. My limitations are too many. I belong to no party, to no organization, political or economic. I come here on the assurance that this is a democratic body which bars the entry of none. I am a man of books and of ideas; if you choose to put it that way I am an intellectual, plain and simple. My sole interest in life is the students' welfare in general and their culture in particular. In fact, I had better tell you straightaway lest you and others to whom my voice may reach misunderstand me or cherish false illusions about me, that I am free to address any group of students on the views about the student community and the present crisis in Indian culture and its future—views which I have formulated to the best of my ability in the course of nearly twenty-five years of educational work. These views are at the disposal of any group of sincere students. The capital presumption of my address, therefore, is the detachment of an intellectual. In case that detachment makes me ruthless, you will pardon me. If again, my training makes me look at the problems of youth in a way different from what you are used to, viz. non-political, and chiefly sociological, you will bear with me. My approach is analytical, and it will be your duty to construct a programme out of that analysis if it appeals to you. I am no leader of men and I am no adviser to youth. Take me merely as a student of affairs, one of you.

Friends, as I said, the general situation in India today is utterly miserable. We have entered the valley of shadows. The light that should come from youthful faces is put out. Let me begin from the class-room, my own immediate arena. What have I noticed there? The enthusiasm of the thirties has faded and the students have become no more than bloodless categories. They are only numbers on the register. They attend lectures, and demand notes and nothing but notes. They are simply interested in getting through examinations and securing jobs. Their intellectual vigilance is at the lowest ebb. And yet, it was not always so. Of course, the average university boy and girl never had a high bump of curiosity or a high tension of awareness. But then, some students were to be found every year who would pull up the standard by a sort of capillary action. I know how difficult it is to buy even the textbooks in the market. Most of them are not available. Those which are set apart in the libraries as textbooks are mutilated, or what is worse, monopolized by a few who do not read them. Formerly, students would form clubs, study-circles and associations of their own. Today, they either do not exist or they are started only to die of desuetude. The unions are not functioning, and no substitutes providing a common platform have been formed. What one occasionally finds is a sectarian body inviting people who are already committed to the views of that body. It is difficult to bring out students' journals in these days of paper restriction. Only three years ago each hostel of my University would bring out at least three issues every year. Now none can secure the quota, with the result that the healthy spirit of emulative creation has been baulked of legitimate expression and directed towards lampooning in the worst possible taste. Sheets go round in which students vilify each other, publish scandals about their class-mates of both sexes and spurt poisonous vituperations against the revered leaders of parties and communities. Most of them are anonymous.

The students of Bengal have suffered most from the paper shortage. Here, literature has been intimately connected with monthly journalism; here, literary activity has been the dominant urge of the youth; here also, more than anywhere else the contribution of the students to literature has been the largest. Some of the poems, stories, essays on literary criticism and on music which I would read about 10, 15, or 20 years ago in purely students' journals bore the royal signature of promise. The latest journals that have come to me are so much waste of paper. Barring one or two poets and short-story writers, the last two years have not produced anything which is worth more than a railway traveller's notice. I refuse to believe that the grand tradition, which Bankim, Michael Madhusudan, Rabindranath so patiently built up with their toil and inspiration, has dried up. No, that's not possible, because traditions die hard. Only, that energy which was institutionalized into a tradition—literature is a major institution in Bengal—has been dammed up, with disastrous consequence in the form of a fairly complete demoralization of the creative faculty.

Friends, please do not be hurt if I tell you to your face that your proverbial idealism has fallen low. On a few counts, and on those alone, for which you do deserve compliment, your idealism has been maintained. I refer primarily to the relief activities in which you have done a magnificent job of work. Along with that you have abolished the barriers of provincialism; and all that you have achieved when the leaders were inside prison, when indifference was wide-spread and the odds against you were high indeed. Another will be mentioned later on. But in other fields your idealism has been reduced to the shouting of slogans. The thinner the conviction the louder is your voice. Those whose ears are close to the ground easily find out that the loudness is of an empty canister. They will not equate it to the voice of the deeps, to the mighty chorus of ground-swells, often muddy, foamy and full of colourful spray, but echoing the music that celebrates the marriage of the elements. What one hears is a dull thud, a whine and a whimper, or at best, the movement of rats over broken glass. I spare you the cross-section of your morals. Your own Chairman of the Reception Committee has spoken about them. In the twenties, the youth went off their moorings, and the world was shocked. But then, that departure represented some reaction against social taboos, some assertion of individuality. It was romantic, nostalgic, sentimental, reckless and often irresponsible; it had no world-view, no ideology as you put it; it had no understanding of the social process; it was urban and petty *bourgeois* at that. But even then, all that was translated into one form of culture or another; even then, all that sensuality was rendered into sensuousness—a necessary ingredient in poetry and music. When all that romantic upsurge was controlled in the thirties, Indian culture entered into a new phase. In Hindi literature, Suman and Narendra were the fresh entrants; in Urdu, Mejaj and Jafri, to name only those I know. Bengali literature produced Sudhindra Datta and Bishnu De among poets, Manik Banerji and Tarashankar among novelists, and a host of minor writers who kept the average high. Why in creative literature alone? In criticism, in music and in painting, the thirties reaped a rich harvest. I am not unaware of the limitations of this period. Its spirit was still unrelated to life; it still remained preoccupied with the little self, and much of its novelty was spurious; in reaction, it adopted values which did not always spring either from the soul or from the soil. Its cult of materialism was often a pose;

its adoption of Marxist terms was often a childish annexation, an adolescent greed and lust. And yet, there was a stubborn core of seriousness, a genuine desire to understand, and a passion for ideas. You take it from me—and I can speak with some confidence on these aspects of our cultural history—that in spite of your protestations that the world is moving ahead, the standard of your creative and critical faculties has gone down. In these years of travail which should have been the years of golden opportunity for the young who are alleged to flourish in crises, in these years you have not thrown up a single writer, a single painter, a single musician who can hold his own against his immediate predecessor. Your best is a section of the old guard who have chosen to continue. All this is tragic. The essence of tragedy is the victimization of values.

And you, with your internecine, fratricidal quarrels are the sacrificers. Only a mathematical God can count the number of student groups, and I know of only one deity, the Goddess Sani, who can measure the mischief that is brewed out of this vintage. And what decency, what honesty, what love of the country you the student body as such, have betrayed! If one group has dared to differ, that group is branded by the other as Fascists, as traitors, spies, and what not! How cheaply are these words bandied about! I wish there were taxes on the abuse of words: Communism, Fascism and Nationalism—the revenue would have been enough for all the reconstruction programmes hatched for the country. And this hatred is not confined to words alone. Here at least theory is wedded to action, and there have been murders of students belonging to one group by those of another. I am not here to fix responsibility. I simply note it with the heaviest of hearts.

When two armies are spoiling for a fight, it does not matter who fires the first shot. More criminal than these murders is the display of hooliganism against girl students. It makes one's blood boil to see bruises, as I have seen, on young girls' heads and arms made by hockey-sticks One can pardon husbands for throwing a dish or two at their wives, say for a badly cooked meal, but these girls are not yet your wives. They are only your class-fellows who have helped their mothers in their drudgery at home, who look after their younger brothers and sisters in the morning and at night, who have joined your college against the still persisting taboos, and who, like you, are picking up new ideas and new contacts. To go at them for difference in political views is worse than obscenity—it is vulgarity.

I have been told by some that all this disintegration is ultimately traceable to the political situation in the country. I am not quite sure about that. The political situation is bad, very bad indeed. The major communities are drifting apart. Suspicion is growing, hatred is mounting. The Hindus among patriots vilify Qaid-e-Azam, a man of incorruptible honesty and unquestioned patriotism, and Muslims among patriots mistrust Gandhiji, the greatest man of the world. All alike suspect British intentions as expressed by the men in power, without the slightest regard to the forces that are being released in Great Britain under the duress of war, forces which are superior to personalities. The deadlock is there, and nobody knows when it is going to end. But then, since when did youth accept the given? Is it not the privilege of youth to change the texture and the course of events? I am told that nearly every young man today is a Socialist. But does Socialism take the objective situation as the primitive man takes the totem? Has Socialism replaced

God and Religion only to put a transcendental History and the 'objective situation' in their stead? This is the old Subjective Idealism staging a come-back; and young men who put it all to the deadlock have yielded to it with the unquestioning faith of a barbarian, a savage.

Is it not up to you all to change it, at least to make an effort to modify it? In 1907, you young men forced the pace of the national movement; in the thirties, at Karachi, you did likewise. You did not then surrender to the situation, you trusted yourselves, and you made history. But today, you are more busy in fighting one another than in making history which to my mind is the meaning of Socialism.

Is not that business of changing the objective situation enough job in your hand? Does it not demand co-operative, collective, deliberate effort? Does it not involve serious study, close analysis, complete, puritanic, ascetic devotion of all groups, irrespective of the shades of differences? Is the colour of your shirts more valuable than the texture of your mind and character? If ever there was any need for unity in your ranks it is now when the political situation is the darkest. Now is the time for cleansing the atmosphere of the smoke, dust and din of borrowed, derivative slogans. The only slogan is Unity in the ranks of the student community. Through Unity in the ranks of the student community alone will you stop the rot that has overtaken you and the country. Stop slogan-shouting, heresy-hunting, traitor-baiting. That's how Germany went to the dogs and sent the world down hurtling into the abyss of violence. For Heaven's sake, please learn the lessons of history. All of you hate Nazism; so don't create it.

Friends, do not think I am partial towards you just because I have been so long diagnosing your pathological condition. I do not exonerate my own tribe. Paralysis has seized us too. Only, in our case it is creeping paralysis which, as Dr B. C. Roy will tell you, is more insidious and almost incurable. We call that disease 'Commonsense', 'caution', 'the scientific attitude'. Of course it has always been with us. We have always been willing to betray, to prostitute our intellect for filthy lucre. And yet, probably, there was a time when a few of us held our heads high. They were the liberals and the humanists, and they stood up for certain values. But to discover their progeny in our midst, one has to use a high power lens. And then one notices on the slide fluttering animalcules gravitating round certain centres and fields of vested interests. Today, our intellectual honesty is below par, which was never very high. Today, we are either white or black, red or blue, but never bright, never incandescent. If a teacher entertains some sincere doubt about the possibility of Socialism in our country in the immediate future, he is a reactionary, and he takes refuge in the vaguest form of mystical economics,—I mean, the economics of the London and Cambridge schools. If a professor is critical of the quality of our nationalism, he is called a spy, and he retreats into his shell of frustration. The net result is that intellectualism today, like love, is either sacred or profane. Here again, I do not blame the individuals of our profession. The times are hard, books and journals are not available, we have to supplement our income by writing piffle, taking tuitions, and in certain cases, I have been told, by other forms of perquisites. I know all that and much more. But what I do not understand is the deterioration in the quality of our scholarship, in the quality of our respect for the students as human beings, in our attitude towards life.

We have become cynics, not realists but just materialists with a few axes to grind. We do not think of our country, we do not think of large issues, we only think of our own advancement in status and salary and we do odd things to catch votes. In other fields, we do not think at all, we just cerebrate. Naturally, the students have caught our disease. Our fates are entangled for good or evil.

What then is the way out? It is almost a desperate situation. But I have not lost hope. I am not a politician, only a teacher of Economics and Sociology, so I cannot throw light on the political problems of the day. As a sociologist I can speak. I detect a few rays of hope. Friends, your work for relief would do any man's heart good. You have broken provincial barriers. I have already spoken about that. In regard to the vexing questions of minorities, I find that you have popularized the idea of social equity, social justice as between classes and communities, and thereby you have sought to improve the quality of our nationalism. If your efforts have not succeeded yet, I do not despair. The seeds of good will are there. You have made people realize the dangers of Fascism. These are solid achievements in the sense that the country will find it awkward to go back on your commitments. But they are not enough. And here is the crux of my address. The reasons for your inadequacy are not political, nor are they economic. They are, in my opinion, basically sociological. I do feel that the essentials of the problems of youth have not been seized either by our leaders or by yourselves. They may have confidence in you, but you have none in yourself. And here is my humble effort to make a contribution to your movement. I repeat, I am no politician, I am no partisan, and my address is meant for all who love and build hopes on the young.

Friends, I shall put before you three fundamental theses about the problems of youth. If you understand them in the right spirit, I feel that you will succeed in evolving a programme with an individuality of its own, not a subversive individuality, but a genuinely co-operative and constructive and creative individuality. I shall categorically state them.

(1) The Indian youth, between 15 and 30, constitute less than 25 per cent of the entire population. As such, they are what I call the *sociological minority*. Elsewhere, as in Soviet Russia, with whose demography India bears some comparison in virtue of the high birth rate and the high rate of increase, as much as 45 per cent of the whole population are under twenty years. The vitality of a society, its capacity for progressive action, its proneness to new ideas and its fervour depend upon the ratio of its youth to the sum of the children and the aged. The factors mainly responsible for this state of affairs are maternal mortality, diseases, and epidemics, each one of which can be effectively controlled. Once they are rightly tackled, the sociological minority can be converted into a majority with all that it means in the way of better, adventurous life. I do not suggest that you should at once get married as a protest against the majority. No, no. The process involves a whole-hearted co-operation with the aims and objects of the Kasturba Memorial Fund and similar societies, and the establishment not only of permanent relief measures but also of preventive ones. Political parties, irrespective of caste, community and ideology, can do nothing better than to accept this national constructive programme laid so clearly by Gandhiji. This is the scientific harnessing of biology to politics to make a better society. No political party, particularly of young men and women,

can afford to ignore Nature. They would do well to exploit her by lifting her functions to the conscious plane by common, deliberate effort. All types of relief works are helpful to improve the status of youthfulness in society.

(2) The youth, as such, are *not* citizens, but only *marginal* beings. On one side, there is the family control, and on the other, the uncertainties of the world—anarchic, pell-mell and uncontrolled. In between come the youth. Those who are students imbibe new, disturbing ideas, others just carry on. The Speciality of the Indian student consists in the fact that in his case while the family control is extremely well defined in its conventions, his economic future is very dark. In Indian colleges and universities, the ideas do not usually spring from the realities of the situation but from old text-books dealing with old-world doctrines, with the result that frustration is usually mixed up with a big dose of historical unreality. Therefore, the Indian student, more than the student of any other country with the exception of China, hovers between a world that is dead and another that is afraid to be born. But it is not always a bad thing. The apprehension of values which can be and has been developed in India is some compensation, and imitation or diffusion is often the starting-point of invention. The problem of youth, therefore, is to cure the unreality of being on the margin. It cannot be solved, in my opinion, from the family side of the issue. The real solution is boldly to look ahead and transform the anarchic future into concrete possibilities. Once this task is enunciated, its performance brings together all sections and parties into the fold of the creative process. Capitalism, even in the shape of controlled public corporations, is not likely to prevent recurring insecurity, and it certainly fails to arouse the enthusiasm

of youth. It perpetuates the marginal man both in theory and practice. But the youth would want to be an integer, continuous and homogeneous. So the youth, as a whole, must work out a planned society to assure the integrity of each individual young. Young men' and women, only by virtue of their being young, cannot plan rightly. They are merely the reservoir of energy, neither good nor bad. The direction and flow of the stream can only be governed by the dynamics of history, for which knowledge is necessary. And knowledge of necessity is freedom.

(3) The young are more than the students. They include the youth in the factories and fields. The problems of the latter are general; and of the former, particular—in so far as they arise out of the economic group to which they belong. That group is only an artificial, urban and specious class. Just as in the two other theses, in case of a conflict between the problems of the sociological minority and of the merely political minority, between those of the whole man and of the marginal man, the larger considerations should prevail and offer grounds of co-operation between all factions and parties, so here also the separation and the opposition between the middle-class student community and the common youth outside the class-room can be solved by emphasizing the superior interests of the larger group, viz. the Indian youth in general, and ultimately the youth of all countries.

The above three theses are usually synthesized by the young themselves in a certain dynamic outlook towards life, an abiding faith in life as a social process and by a highly tense awareness. However dim its outline, its content, urge and direction are defined by the will of the young to transform their status of minority and marginality and to remove their social distance from the rest of society by organizing a vigorous students' movement. This has been partly done in our country since 1936 when the student community formed themselves into an organization for the first time. Its motive power was supplied by the national movement which had then entered into a new phase. But mainly its motive power. That power was strong in the strength of its assertion of national dignity, its idea of service to the country, its search for social justice, and its deep commitments to the interests of democracy. In short, your movement has been a part of the national movement. It was very natural, in fact necessary to a large extent. What, however, has happened, in that process of identification is that the youth movement has been swallowed up in the national movement, with the result that it has partaken of its deficiency even if it has shared in its merit and gloried itself in the reflected light. Here again, pardon me if I am wrong in my analysis. I speak as an outsider. Our national movement has been trying to reach the people, but I sometimes think that its concept of the people is still romantic. The people today are still a crowd, and not a social and economic category, having no hold over the means of production and the conditions of their livelihood. I also think that in spite of the best efforts, the national movement has not made the vital distinction between (i) the nationhood of nationalism which, to my mind, was the joint product of a reaction against the domination of the Western civilization and a new type of Renaissance based on a sort of protestant dignity and self-respect, and (ii) the nationhood of nationalities such as arose in Gujerat, Maharashtra, Bengal, Oudh, in every region of India in reaction against the Central authority of the Pathans and

Mughals at Delhi. Each such nationality developed a cultural pattern of its own. Bengal formed her own literature, music, painting and architecture. So did Gujerat. And it was not quite a bad thing. When the Delhi authority wanted to further centralize, the Mughal Empire decayed. Then came the East India Company and transformed the social economy of these regions one by one; and the hope of a multi-formal unity of Indian life, its organic plurality of selves, was extinguished. The thing that came was the concept of an impersonal, abstract national unity, which was in the nature of a reply to, a psychological support and ballast of the administrative unity which the British Government had achieved. This decay of concrete nationality gives a hollow ring to our modern Indian culture. When Bengal was partitioned, the pain and sorrow were real, the response in culture was genuine. I wonder if the phrase or the danger of vivisection of India can really create the same response in the heart of Indians who say that the unity of Indian culture is built into their bones. At least, I am waiting for it.

So, friends, I have come to the end of my address. As an intellectual, my soul writhes in agony at the disintegration of Indian culture, at your inability, which I hope is a temporary deficiency, to give it new shape and content. As a teacher, a well-wisher of youth, as one who has come to the end of his days, I beseech you to unite in order that the rot may be stopped. Let not a single unkind word slip out of your tongue and pen. Unite you must, for the stakes are no less than the future of your status and function as youth and the future of your country. Seek knowledge, its unity, its history, and its process in all devotion, in what Leonardo da Vinci called obstinate rigour. Go and tell your teachers of the

Humanities to be human by relating knowledge to the evolution of society, to the functions of living. Ask your teachers of science to tell you its history and its social implications. Make them work hard, exploit their specialized knowledge. Outside the sanctum, continue your social service, not only in the towns but in the villages. Give new content to the meaning of nationalism. Fill it with social justice, equity to all classes and communities. And above all, study the social forces with discrimination. Loudness is no substitute for earnestness Be grim and bare. Touch the bones of the problems, and you will give them flesh and blood, you will breathe into them the secret of life. You are capable of all that and much more. I am sure of it. Lastly, think if the theses I have propounded about the problems of youth in general are not the right ones. They are my analysis, and I do not suggest that you should gulp it. I do not want to impose anything on you. But you cannot do justice to it if it is right, unless you unite by closing up your ranks. So I plead for Unity.

Unity first, unity second, unity last—a whole sequence, a whole series of Unities, is the evolving design of the life that is dawning upon the world. Just see what is happening in the distant corners. The forces of liberation are on the march, and the march is in a quick tempo. If you don't look out, they will leave you high and dry. Will you deny yourselves the vigour of a changing world? Will you be taken unawares when the opportunity which you and we of the older generation have been waiting for is just within reach? That will be the supreme betrayal of the Human Spirit.

2. SOCIOLOGY OF THE INDIAN YOUTH.

Young Friends,

Your connexion with politics has been close for well over a quarter of a century by now. Every dispassionate observer of Indian affairs knows that you have thrown yourselves into the various political movements which have enriched the content of our national consciousness. If sometimes you have been moved by what old men and the powers that be call 'passion', on other occasions your action has been prompted by convictions. But in no case have your motives been unworthy. The country has every cause to be grateful to you for your political services. And the expression of that gratitude by our leaders has been fulsome. You have been called the future leaders of the country, the architects of its fortune, the repository of all noble impulses; you have been asked to give up your studies and sacrifice your time, energy and prospects, to wage the struggle and act as its spearhead; and from every convocation address and political meeting you have returned with redoubled confidence and some complacency.

Unfortunately, however, your economic achievements have not been quite on par with your considerable political feats. I must say, however, that very few of us have obliged you in your efforts at economic betterment. When you have approached the leaders, you have been fobbed off by earnest advice to go back to the land and spin there, reconstruct villages, or do 'social service'. We teachers have given you certificates and recommendations, knowing fully that they are worse than useless to the head of a Government department or to any large-scale employer. The latter has often been rude to you telling you to your face that a university training has made you unfit for life by instilling a false dignity into your green mind; and he has often wound up that frank and friendly talk by holding himself up as your model of what a non-university man with sufficient 'character and honesty' can do in this ruthless world of competition. Meanwhile, your guardians have been pestering you to go and get a job and lend them your assistance to shoulder the ever-growing burden of maintaining the family, the why of which you cannot of course enquire if you are decent. The story of your economic advance is not a particularly bright one. In fact, it is as sombre as the story of your political achievement is brilliant.

Why should there be a contrast between these two aspects of your activity? Is Indian life such a sharp chiaroscuro? Should politics be so tonelessly separated from economics? What on earth prevents you from offering your total selves for the all-round betterment of India, and incidentally, the enhancement of your own income? The answers are well known; but they are no more definitive than those which are given in reply to the problems of your political or even intellectual frustration. Foreign rule, imperialism, capitalism, objective situation are only partial answers. You have accepted their challenge in the political field. Is economic exploitation then more insidious, more pervasive than political subjection? But then, all sections of Indian youth agree that politics in India precedes Indian economics. That may or may not be correct, but how long can a single, individual young Indian hold out against odds? Independence may or may not come; if it comes at all, it is likely to come late. Then may some young men feel that it has come too late. They will have become family men by then, with a number of rickety children and a sickly, nagging wife, *plus* a few self-sacrificing widowed aunts and sisters, to support. If the youth can stay the course of Indian family life, so far so good. If they cannot, nobody can blame them. All that can be said about them is that they were realists enough to perceive that while youth as such was a succession of generations, their own youth had broken with a crash into middle age and what it means in the way of family responsibilities. After all, realism is a natural mood which co-exists with the spirit of idealism; after all, individual life is also an item in the procedure of general living; after all, the idea of political autonomy may ultimately behave like any other god, demanding blood and sacrifice and giving poor substitutes in return. Surely, politics and economics cannot be thus divorced in the lifetime of an individual. One must conclude that the leaders' and the elders' approach to the problems of youth has been sidewise. Undoubtedly, your problems are intimate with the political sovereignty and the economic advance of India. But they are much more.

The proper approach to the problems of youth is sociological. Sociology, you should know, is not just Social Reform or Social Welfare. Nor is it a hodge-podge of social sciences like Economics and Politics. It has a scope of its own and has a very rigorous discipline. Its point of view subsumes the sectional ones; its laws' or generalizations or universal hypotheses—give them any name you like so long as you don't use metaphors—bind economic behaviour, political events and juridical principles; its vision is thus all-comprehensive. So the sociological approach does not commit the crime of splitting up the youth into distinct groups of young men and women, then subdividing them into separate atoms, and ultimately pitting each of them against one another and against society, in artificial situations of conflict. In the sociological understanding, conflict is one form of relation, individual is one form of personality, group is one form of society organization. Nor would a sociologist look at the problems of youth merely as cross-sections of the Indian problem; he would study them in the context of social development which, incidentally, he knows to be amenable to very systematic treatment. Beyond this we cannot at present define the sociological approach. You will have an idea of it in the course of this talk on your problems. By the way, do not expect solutions of problems from a professor. How can we solve any problem of life when we have done our best to avoid it by becoming teachers and professors? Please also do not forget that we are not here discussing the solutions in the shape of practical programmes. We are concerned with the nature of your problems and the proper approach towards them.

Youth does not exhaust the number of boys and girls taking college education. The term 'youth' is statistical and includes all those who come under the age-category of say 15 to 25. So the men and women working in fields and factories must needs come into that category of population. Those who enjoy unearned income and inherited wealth are children. Gainful occupation and its search are the two tests of this group. College students only form one section creating one or two special problems of their own, for example, those which arise from the mixture of sentimental attitude of guardians with cynical interference in their wards' life. This section forms as it were 'a class', although it is a spurious class suffering from a sense of difference or social distance from other sections of the age-group. One peculiarity of this comprehensive group of 15-25 is the statistical fact that just at the moment when the outer limit, i.e. the age 25, is going to be crossed, the expectation of life is practically nil. Only the other day, the expectation of life at 24 years was under 25, except in Madras—probably as a concession to the genius for the science of numbers which Madras is reputed to possess. Anybody who has looked at an average Indian woman of 25 should know that statistics do not always lie. For her, youthfulness is 'literature'.

One important consequence of the short-lived nature of Indian youth is that while the quantity of population may merrily increase, as it is doing now, the quality of that increase is poor. Quantitatively, we all want our society to be dynamic and progressive, at least, for some years to come. From the point of view of its vitality a population that has at least an equal proportion between the youth on the one hand and the children and the aged on the other is desirable. In India, the infants and the old rule. We have more infants and old people than we can afford. Just think of the widows and the doddering men over 70 reported in the Census. They are estimable creatures; but don't you think that their pull is socially backward?

Of course, sex is an important problem for the young. But not quite in the way in which you, the students, take it. For you, it is an urge all right; but one wonders if it, as you feel it, is not an anti-social thing. Sex-urge is not equal to marriage in your case. This is not true for other sections of your age-group. There sex-instinct surrenders itself into marriage and marriage fades into family. At no stage of social development has physiological adolescence exactly synchronized with social adolescence. That gap has only increased in the student-group's case, thanks mainly to economic pressure. It has given rise to numerous complications with which a particular type of literature has made us familiar, and which, to be honest, that literature has done its best to foster and confuse. Of all the progeny of predicaments which the students' sex-urge has created, the worst is the concept of Love. Students by themselves could not have begotten it, but our effeminate literature has always been helpful. This conspiracy of literature (music, painting, cinema too—they are adjuncts to literature in our country) with the sex-urge of the middle-class youth has been responsible for a host of substitute feelings and attitudes which hang over the mind like a smoke-screen. The first duty of students towards their sex, therefore, is to see through that veil. And the best way of doing it seems to be to question the primacy of sex itself for the youth as a whole. The British connexion has brought a number of social evils to India, but the worst of them is this *bourgeois*-liberal-individualistic-romantic view of sex as the sole bond between a Rai Bahadur's son and a Rajah Saheb's daughter, now a sweeper's adopted girl according to our progressive cinema. The Indian youth, if they were true to themselves, would give the palm to fear, particularly the fear of insecurity and grinding poverty. If it were not so, the slow postponement of the age of marriage in the course of the last two or three decades would remain inexplicable. Probably, you would not agree. But surely, you would not object if I maintain that the development of individuality by the acquisition of status and the due discharge of functions in society wrests the primacy from sex as the main social drive of youth. Mating as such is not much of a social problem. Marriage and family are. Sex-urge is only one form of the social energy of which the Youth are the store. Even then, civilization has gone ahead by controlling it, and particularly, in our country.

If, therefore, the more or less complete subordination of sex to marriage and of marriage to family and of family to a larger social grouping be the cardinal fact of Indian society, then the problems of Indian Youth should nucleate round that fact of subordination. Subordination means law, code, order, pressure, control, none of which is pleasant. In other words, your problems arise in the lag or the gap between adolescence and social initiation, i. e. active membership of the society. Now, up till adolescence, the young person has no independent social existence of his own. All that he knows is a series of don'ts. At adolescence he is a member of the family, his guardian's ward, feeling the rigours of protection. If he lives in a hostel away from his parents or works in a factory, there is some chance for his rebel side to develop. But the student goes back home after his degree, marries the girl of his guardian's choice and is taken along with the bride unto the bosom of Abraham. And then abandon all hope, ye that enter here'. If the young man gets a job far away he proposes to take his wife and the baby, but then the mother disposes. Thus the family tradition is perpetuated, the adult remaining a replica of the father and expecting his wife to eternally mother him. The girl's case is much worse. Only the young labourer in the city can occasionally afford to be free from the family influence. It is no exaggeration to say that the family conditioning of the young man and the woman is the chief source of all that mess which goes by the name of marriage. Of course, it is the romantic-individualistic-liberal-*bourgeois* marriage. But that is the type you consider to be ideal and for which you are getting ready by acquiring all the appropriate silly notions about love, life and culture.

Now the socially desirable thing about it all is the discontent implicit in your urge for individuality. One would not like to panegyrize it by calling it divine. You want to get away from your guardians and be a unit. But there are two anti-social implications of your desire. First, yours is a freedom *from*, not a freedom *to*; in fine, it is a negative wish. The impulse of freedom is no guarantee for being autonomous, just as a free nation in the sense of freedom *from* foreign yoke need not imply a nation of free men. Unless the positive content of freedom is there beyond the corner, the spirit of rebellion may as well waste itself in orgies of destruction or of suicide at the feet of dictators. From the father to the dictator is not a difficult step. The two belong to the same genus. Secondly, even when you do not succumb to dictatorship or to militarism in order to hide your isolation, loneliness, helplessness, you may still continue to be negative. Protestantism is a virtue suited to an age. It loses its adequacy in another when constructive planning is called for. The popular governments did magnificent work in the three years of their rule. At the beginning, however, the very natural difficulty of a change-over from the critical attitude, rendered habitual by the political disposition, into one of constructive endeavour occasioned even by that partial autonomy, had to be faced. Much of the opposition to the C. R. formula comes from this critical tradition, just as that series of bureaucratic futilities known as reconstruction plans are ultimately traceable to Mr Amery's 'No, Sir's'.

The young are undoubtedly less amenable to the spell of negation than their elders, yet its dangers should not be minimized. And the chief one is frustration which being an interference with the occurrence of response at its proper time in behaviour-sequence takes the form of aggression in action and cynicism in cerebration.

So it comes to this: The young have the 'from'-attitudes well developed, but not the 'to'-attitudes in which they are at the mercy of affectionate but unthinking elders and vendors of exciting shibboleths. The strength of youth is in their vast store of energy and in their not being affiliated to vested interests. Being marginal men, they can thus travel quickly and lightly. But the direction is not in their hands. Please remember what happened to the German Youth Movement. Hitler canalized it for Fascist purposes. On the other hand, the Chinese youth forged the unity of China. Youth as such is no more good or bad than say petroleum is. It is only a reservoir of energy. The point, therefore, is the sense of direction. Who will give it? Leaders? Leaders can build the banks of the canal through which your energy will flow. But do leaders create the bed of the canal, the incline and the quality of the soil and all that which facilitates the main flow fairly independently of the banks and the side-walls? Do they raise the level of the sub-soil water? Some are reputed to have done so. But they have special gifts, a sense of history, combined with a complete understanding of the social realities. Mere contact with the people, finger on their pulse, prestige, spell, charm, sacrifice are not sufficient. They must understand the social forces in terms of laws of social development. They must be sociologists in this sense first and last. They are a very rare specimen. Who can wait for their emergence? Far better would it be if the youth understood by themselves the nature and development of social forces. They will throw up leaders from their own ranks. Please do not have any illusions about 'understanding'. It is a very hard job. It means intensive study and action in perfect combination. It means anything but shouting like empty canisters.

To what extent a close contact with the social reality can transform the energy that is youth has been made clear by what the young have done in Bengal. Poverty, large-scale poverty, mass poverty, is India's first social reality. What had so long passed as poverty was its rumour. Poverty is not the economic insecurity of the middle-class graduate who has at least his mother's or wife's ornaments to fall back upon. But genuine poverty is sub-human, bestial, brutal. It does not only mean living on grass—some grasses have vitamins. It means the father and mother selling their daughters for [illegible] apiece. It means the peasant selling his single head of cattle to the butcher for a rupee. And it is not confined to one case or two. Such things happened in Bengal on a large scale. During relief the young men of India saw the basic reality for the first time And it was the finest shock-therapy on record. They went into the villages, and saved a few millions. The accredited leadership was in jail, others were indifferent, or making money. So the youth threw up leaders from their own ranks the moment they understood the capital social reality of starvation. Please note the difference. In our days, we also did relief-work. But we were philanthropists. Later on, some of us went about doing social welfare. This time, however, it was not the usual relief. It was creative work, revolutionary effort, and hence it meant a new birth. Have you talked with these people who have come back from Bengal and Malabar? They are new specimens of humanity. Are they Bengalis, Punjabis, Madrasis? Where is that middle-class product, provincialism? Are they Hindu students, Muslim students, Depressed Class students? They are just the youth of India. And the girls? Are they the delicate jasmine stalks whom our poets describe and artists paint in soulful abandon and whom you want to love and you will rue if you will marry? These new girls are Damascus blades. Have you listened to what they talk about the future of our society? They are democrats to a person. And their democracy is not negative, but very positive.'

Please do not misunderstand the position. Bengal cannot always thus oblige the youth of India. And yet Bengal's position is not unusual. Most Indians live on nature's level, which is the sub-human level. That level is the first social reality. Some have understood it, others have not. You must all seize it at once and transmute your behaviour towards it into a social force in accordance with the first law of social evolution, viz. the conversion of action into function. Once that function gets going the positive content of freedom takes shape. After all, democracy posits the integration of social functions operating through groups, and the largest group consists of the Indian mass living on the sub-human level. The first problem of Indian youth is to be conscious of its existence in Indian life. Once that is done, its function has to be understood in the context of social dynamics. Afterwards? Then you will no longer be young. Others will take your place to lift the social functioning into higher levels of creation.

Thus it is that the sociological approach to the problems of youth is not merely one of discovering your proportion to the total population or a due appreciation of the implications of your sex-urge. They are relevant but not essential. Nor is that approach concerned only with your quest for individuality, which is only a *versus* relation to society. It is not even the discovery of your fund of energy. Even this freedom is only half the approach. A full sociological vision embraces social reality which is the life of the people as it is lived; a sociological approach means the discovery of the ways and means to convert the status of the people into social functioning. But then it will be a different society, viz. the democratic. But it cannot be helped.

3. INDIAN YOUTH THE MARGINAL BEING

Youth is a 'Marginal' conception. Young men and women, in so far as they are human, cannot be reduced, however, to the status of the marginal being. Hence the perpetual conflict between Youth and Age, the story of which ranges from the residential segregation of primitive tribes to the tension of ideologies in civilized communities.

The marginality of Youth arises in various ways. *Psychologically*: The transition from childhood to manhood is violently broken by the irruption of sex. The reflexes and habits which have been more or less stabilized by now are rudely disturbed by sex which first scatters them into the generalized state of a novel awareness, and then would seek to focus them into the point of a personality with an interest all its own. Now the attitude is no longer of acceptance but of uncertainty. Adolescent Youth is no more sure. He has passed from the family's given pattern to the adventure of annexing the new. Old habits are of little avail, old relations do no more obtain, but the new ones are not yet fixed. The object of love is for the first time objective, outside the subject, and she or he demands subjection. If the Youth belong to the aggressive type by virtue of his upbringing, the object must needs be subjected. This process is as romantic as that of self-surrender which is only a variation of the desire to continue the old attitude of accepting the given and the fixed relations. Among the primitive tribes this period of tension is shortened

1. *Vide*, Karl Mannheim: *Diagnosis of Our Time*.

by licensed intercourse; with older civilizations it is done by early marriage; in rural communities, the technique is the same; but for the modern Youth, the period is prolonged. The advantage which the urban young enjoy in the shape of greater opportunities for intercourse is chiefly counterbalanced by two factors: (*a*) the prolongation of the protected period of childhood and its consequences in the ignorance of vital matters and preoccupation with the pleasure-aspects of contact; and (*b*) the aversion from familial responsibility, heightened, among other factors, by the wider choice of possibilities and the greater sense of insecurity. The net result is that the young person is dislodged from his fortress of stability and yet is not in possession of the chances of forming or growing into another order of permanence. In short, he is at the margin of two levels of social existence, both mainly familial, but one pre-sexual and the other post-sexual, one with values determined by social traditions and taken without question, the other with values in the making of which he feels that he should occasionlly have a share when the choice of the partner is made. Such discontinuity from one level to another is the essence of marginality.

These are general considerations. The peculiarity of the Indian Youth's case consists in the fact that while the pre-sex setting is rigidly fixed by family conventions, the post-sex setting is felt to be, and really is, highly speculative. Choice of the partner is not customary; ideas almost hostile to old values are imbibed in schools and colleges; new values cannot be realized; only the structure of ideas crashes. The Indian Youth's marginality is thus only more tragic. In addition to sex, he has the whole range of ideas about love and freedom to make life discontinuous, and with little or no chance to bridge the gulf. He is thus separated from his family-conventions by two sets of forces instead of one, and when he starts his family-life he discovers to his dismay that the new life's setting is no better than the old, with only the memory of its prospects intervening like the ghost of a suicide. So the tragedy of the Indian Youth is of the romantic variety. His agony of being on the margin of frustration is none the less real for that. He is a dreamer with no hope of waking up to any fresh scheme of reality.

Economically : The young are ever on the margin of economic security everywhere, except in one area—the U.S.S.R. So long as they are at school, their guardians pay. When they leave school they search for jobs. In industrialized countries, occupations are varied and staggered. Even then, the fear of unemployment is haunting them. They cannot conquer it, because they cannot pin it down to this factor or that. The fear is impersonal, because the cause of unemployment is impersonal. And yet the young worker sweats and toils very personally, and for real persons, his wife and child; his losing the job has very personal consequences. Somebody high up in the directorate, one whom he may or may not have seen, miscalculates; something has happened somewhere, a war, the birth of a new company, a new invention, and his little world of security falls to the ground; the child coughs, the wife nags and whines, the drink bill mounts. He does not understand it, but he seeks knowledge from which he is barred. If he is a member of a trade union in a free country, he gets some benefit or dole. He turns to socialism; but he meets dull or active opposition from his union bureaucracy and the State. He is fobbed off by cheap explanations; he succumbs, and becomes a nationalist.

With the active assistance of a military State the wires of which are pulled by trusts and combinations, he begins to believe in planning without caring for its means and ends, and he becomes a nationalist *and* a socialist, in short, a Nazi. Not always, however; sometimes, the young worker does understand, and then he believes in his role, the role of his class. Then he is apt to realize that the economic category of class overlaps the sociological category of Youth. Socialism is the attempt of Youth to convert its marginality into continuous integrity. The old cannot be socialists. Herein lies the danger of socialism. The young of today are the old of tomorrow, and so socialism tends to gravitate towards bureaucracy, the structure of the secure and the respectable. At the same time, as a social demographic process, Youth *per se* is never the same. You cannot be young twice, just as you cannot bathe twice in the same stream. The constant pull of the current of living, however, makes the appeal of socialism eternal for the Youth at the margin of stability.

This situation of youthful marginality has been recognized by the sociologists of America in particular. The 'hobo', the wastrel, the vagabond's anti-social potentialities have been duly studied. But the approach suffers from serious defects. It is still mainly pathological. While the juvenile delinquent is no longer treated like a case in a hospital, even the most honest diagnostician fights shy of going to the roots of the problem and tracing delinquency to the frustration of the marginal being and his inhibitions by the impersonal impediments of a system of production which socializes him at one stage and at another de-socializes him, individuates him, splits him up as an earner-consumer haunted by the fear of insecurity. The result is that the sociologist's solution is hopelessly inadequate. He hides his head under the sands of scientific sociology and divests himself of any responsibility for preventing the conditions of juvenile delinquency. Economics is an older science. Its analysis is more rigorous. It is purer, more logical, more abstract, more conceptual, more intellectual, and more unreal. It has frankly accepted the situation as it is. Economics is more neutral, i. e. more irresponsible, than sociology. Only, the economic approach is *not* pathological, not empirical, but a technique of thought, 'an apparatus of thinking', a branch of logic or mathematics! All *bourgeois* economists sense the importance of the margin. They take the marginal producer, consumer, labourer, as the critical determinant of the process of market evaluation. In the next step of distillation, the human factor evaporates, and the marginal revenue, the marginal productivity, the marginal this or that remains. The later stage throws up the concept of the margin as such, marginal time, etc., very similar to T. S. Eliot's point of intersection between the eternal series and the finite sequence. No wonder that the young man ever unhappy at being on the margin and ever ready to end his marginality, does not as a student take kindly to the Marginal School of Economics and plunges headlong into socialism, the economics of which do not thus split him up into segments, each hanging in the air. But then professors do not tell the young that socialism demands serious study. To teach in a way that militates against the psychology of Youth is known as sound pedagogics. Or, is it only fit and proper to teach the principles of economic insecurity, called classical or academic economics, to the young whose future is nothing but uncertain?

The Indian student scores a point or two here against his opposite number in an industrialized society. Margin or no margin, his educational expenses are always borne by his guardians who often mortgage their property against a university degree which is the passport to security, viz. a government job. In case the young graduate fails to get it, he is not thrown to the wolves, but retained by the guardians in the bosom of the family. Why he alone? He, with his wife and a few children too. The Indian Youth who is not a student, but a helper of his family in the fields shares the insecurity of agriculture and of the fluctuations of world prices. In the factories, his tenure of security is nearly as good or bad as elsewhere, with this difference—that his level of income is inordinately low, his technical training is nil, the choice of occupations severely limited, and his employment is really speaking under-employment even though his employment is relieved by assistance from other members of the family. Reference has been made to the complications introduced by sex and new ideas in the life of the marginal youth as an Indian student. He is at a disadvantage as against the young labourer and peasant. Shelley, Keats, and Byron are not read by men and women in the fields and factories of India. That may be an argument against India's fitness for independence, or even dominion status, but it has kept down suicide-figures for the Indian Youth, a term more comprehensive than the student community of India.

The young themselves have so long sought to cure their marginality by falling in love with persons and ideas, in short, by Faith or Idealism. They seem to have thought that they would be lifted thereby from their precarious perch and put firmly on the other side of the gulf on the Rock Abiding. Faith as such, how-even sells at a discount today. But the urge towards continuity and integrity is all there, and it is very real. After the last war, the Young became disillusioned. The Cause they were asked to fight for was exposed as a conspiracy. So some swung to World Revolution. Trotsky begot a brood of dreamers. The defeated nations and the new ones cultivated self-respect. On the Continent, a new Youth movement was started. It was intensely national. In China, in India, in Iran, in Arabia, in Egypt, the Youth wanted to drown their marginality in a *national movement.* It was quite natural, because the cure, the antithesis of discontinuity, of fragmentariness, of marginality, is a movement that is a continuing social process. In India, it has been very natural. Here, the Youth as such has been in the forefront of the national struggle, since the days of the Swadeshi movement. Before that, Indian politics were the concern of the elders, because the national movement itself was staid and respectable, liberal and reformist, very constitutional. When the cry of 'Swaraj is our birthright' was raised, the Youth took it up with great fervour. But they had to wait long before the meaning of Swaraj took recognizable shape. In the meantime, the emotions got a chance, self-sacrifice at the altar of Mother India was expected to do the duty of an integrating force. Martyrdom did light up a fire. It was, however, to be quenched by its own embers. The Youth movement of those days, however, succeeded in making the Indian National Congress realize that political mendicancy would not do. What should do was not clear to anybody. In the next phase of the struggle, the Youth came as followers rather than as the vanguard. Gandhiji sought to transform the fruitless dogma of violence into fruitful non-violent non-co-operation in which the constructive element was formed by a fairly comprehensive programme ranging from education to the charkha *via* the removal of many social disabilities. Two important departures were made in the character of the national movement: (*a*) For the first time, the Muslims were sought to be brought into the fold, and (*b*) attention was turned towards rural India and the people, including the so-called untouchables. Although some fine work was done by the Indian Youth on the constructive side, the Youth movement, as such, did not yet emerge. Nor was there any recognition by anybody, including the student body, of the world forces which opposed the above two departures. There had been a Renaissance among Muslims in the Middle East, and the idea of nationality based upon territorial and cultural homogeneity was spreading fast. Here the ideal of nationalism was oblivious of the above considerations, and it covered the contradiction between extra-territorial allegiance to the Khilafat—itself a dying issue in its homeland—and the territorial patriotism and self-sufficiency of India. Simultaneously, capitalism was facing a crisis in Europe and America, and each State was following restrictionist, protectionist and autarchic policies. In India, capitalism was on the upgrade. It had to be national. But this nationalism was of a different order from that of nationalist Europe. Although much of Indian nationalism was of the neo-mercantilist type, it still retained a world-outlook. One is often surprised at the international viewpoint of the leaders of India in the midst of her intensest national fight. For which thanks are mainly due to Tagore and Jawaharlal. Gandhiji's view of the destiny of man, as distinct from that of the world, was extremely helpful. With these new qualities of the national movement, the Indian Youth could not but be in sympathy.

The next phase of the national struggle in the early thirties established for the first time a living contact with the people. Their economic difficulties had been appreciated, but not properly understood. When the questions of rent and wages came up, Youth had the first glimmer of the positive content of nationalism. Socialism was in the air; the Soviet had started planning and was delivering the goods. Jawaharlal popularized socialism. The movement of the thirties was over, but it left a rich precipitate. Now was the time for the Youth movement to find its own feet. And it did—in 1936. Next year, the Congress assumed office, and leftist forces grew as never before. The marginal being at least enjoyed the change of being a whole.

Unfortunately for the Indian Youth movement, the opportunity did not last long. The Congress withdrew from office; the Cripps offer was rejected; Hindus and Muslims drifted apart; the Pakistan Resolution was passed; the Congress resolutions on minorities and fundamental rights were either forgotten or found inadequate by the Muslims; the Muslim League grew from strength to strength. Rural development programme, Basic Education scheme, almost every nation-building activity which could enthuse the Young was either curtailed or stopped. Labour movement became an impossibility. At this fateful juncture, the August Resolution was passed. Many young people seized it with eagerness. There was no means of knowing if the leaders really wanted an open rebellion. Some thought so, others did not. Both groups, as young men and women, and in the absence of leaders, wanted to further the national cause. But the emphasis was different. One group took its stand upon the immediate, the other upon the possibility. It was like medieval schoolmen arguing about the meaning of nature in Aristotle's dictum about man, whether it should be nature as it is or as it should be. To put it in another way, the difference hinged on whether the lotus should be called *pankaja*, that which rises from mud, or *padma*, the bud. In any case, the Youth movement is today split up into two warring camps, each intolerant of the other with a zeal worthy of a better cause. The urge of the marginal being to be a whole man is suspended, unless it be that mutual hatred is a good substitute for a movement in the service of Youth's integrity and continuity. If hatred were enough, then Gandhiji's whole life has been defeated, then Jawaharlal's chief contribution to Indian politics has been nullified, then the drive of Youth to be a whole man by charging the national movement with new movement, with new meaning is just a fancy and flutter. The blunt truth about the present status and function of the Youth movement is that it only acts as a mirror for the stalemate. And yet it need not be so. During the famine, the students took the lead, did magnificent work, and they are still doing it. They abolished provincial barriers. They pointed out the menace of Fascism. And all wanted the Congress and the League to come together. Only the blind will not see these solid achievements of the Indian Youth. Unfortunately, there are blind people in our midst. They pass judgement and take sides without realizing that all groups of students are young, that Youth has problems of its own, that one of its major problems is to overcome its marginality, that the techniques of doing it are really one in the unity of that basic objective. One fails to understand those who judge the conduct of Youth in terms other than its own. Surely, the Youth movement is an integral part of the national movement. But Youth is *also* Youth, each one at the margin of childhood and adulthood, of set conventions and uncertain values and insecurity. Should not the Young come together on the level of youthfulness and studentship ? What about Indian culture ? Is it not worth some hard thinking and high seriousness ?

4. INDIAN YOUTH IN URBAN SETTING

Every year, at the beginning of the session, I make a little experiment with my students. After explaining the terms, I ask them a few questions on their connexion with 'village life' and on the 'economic group to which they and their guardians belong. As my purpose is not to write a dissertation but only to establish personal contacts with the students and make them feel at home with new subjects like Economics and Sociology, I make my queries very informal and keep the answers loose. And yet, certain broad conclusions have emerged which by their recurrence over a long stretch of years no less than by the support they have received from other sources are worthy of serious consideration in any discussion on the problems of Indian Youth. Our students are becoming dissociated from the countryside and being urbanized in the process. They come under what is loosely called the 'middleclass'.

The urbanization of Youth is part of a larger movement. In spite of a few opposing tendencies, the shift of Indian population has been on the whole from the countryside towards centres of large aggregation. The attraction of mass and cash has proved superior to the virtues of rural life. In the villages, congestion is pretty high, amenities to which even the most unsophisticated of villagers look forward in these days are lacking, the weight of traditions is heavy, the hold of the tentacles of land-tenure is fast and long, and the standard of living is quite often below the level of subsistence. On top of these, economic agencies, like the more than partial conversion of kind-economy into cash-economy, changes in the structure of consumption, the slow but sure industrialization which for its dependence upon the rural areas for raw materials and labour cannot but throw the old economy out of gear, etc.—all these directly and indirectly operate to facilitate mass-migration into towns and cities. Indian economy as it has evolved during this war is more likely to heighten the tempo of this process than not. In such an evolving context, the so-called 'middleclass' is likely to be still more urbanized. Naturally, the urban traits of students are also likely to be more pronounced.

Any modern textbook on Rural and Urban Sociology will give us the distinguishing features of the two worlds, the city and the countryside. Pitrim Sorokin thus describes them in his *Principles of Rural-Urban Sociology*:

(1) In the Urban World, the totality of people are engaged principally in manufacturing, mechanical pursuits, trade, commerce, professions, governing and other non-agricultural occupations'. The first two items are not so important in India as they are in industrialized countries. Trade and commerce are also usually of a small scale. But the liberal professions, including clerkship, form a relatively larger proportion, particularly in the distribution of national income, than elsewhere. While in colleges and schools of certain parts of India one notices the number of students belonging to purely agricultural groups to be creeping up, its progress in the Lucknow University is not marked.

(2) In the cities, there is 'greater isolation from nature', with all that it means in the way of 'the predominance of man-made environment over natural'. Fortunately for the student community in India, excepting in the big cities, the divorce from nature is not complete. The campuses are almost always beautifully situated, and

one often hears the cuckoo in the midst of a lecture on Keynes' Theory of Employment. But what one simultaneously observes is the utter indifference of the students to the grandeur of ancient trees, the play of sunlight on green lawns and the shimmer of dreaming minarets against the sky-line. The susceptibility of adolescence to human beauty is understandable, but seldom is even that beauty natural today. Chemistry has taken a hand. *Basant* and *Holi* come and go without a stir in the youth's sensibilities, and colour is seldom to be seen except in ties and shirts. Girls have almost given it up to avoid attention and in the sacred name of respectability. This is about Lucknow. To my mind, this 'isolation from nature' has been largely responsible for the emotional immaturity of the urbanized youth, a fact to which any teacher of poetry, particularly of the Romantic School, will testify. It is a bad day for India when *Meghaduta* fails to excite the young men and women of India, as it has certainly done in the opinion of friends qualified to speak.

A much subtler mischief than this emotional desiccation has taken place in the general attitude of the young. Contact with nature slowly impregnates the mind with the facts of birth, growth, decay and organic connexion. It habituates one to the patience of years, the large rhythm of cycles and the generosities of corporate existence. In the cities, temporal rhythm is not set by green yielding to auburn, but by Greenwich overriding the psychological tempo, and flattening it. Its inevitability and its desirability from the point of view of historical, economic and political considerations are no compensation for any loss in the sense of growth and of large intervals. Occasionally, one feels that the susceptibility of our youth to changing fashions and to the ideologies of 'crisis' is more due to their urban setting and the resulting divorce from nature than to their youthfulness and foreign propaganda. The great beauty of the Santiniketan experiment in education mainly consists in the re-establishment of nature in the life of pupils. Schemes of Basic Education are directed towards the same end It should be clear, however, that schools and colleges of Agriculture which Government plans envisage are not enough to restore nature in the heart of youth and make it instinct with her lessons and her beauty.

(3) On account of a greater proportion of migrant recruits from fairly distant parts and a greater social differentiation, the urban population is more heterogeneous than the rural. If we add to it the facts that the social pyramid in the cities is higher and their vertical mobility is more intense than in the villages, then we can easily understand the reasons for the decay in community-feeling and the birth of secondary and substitute groups which flourish under the sense of marked differences. Cities are abodes of contrasts. They do, therefore, sharpen the edge of consciousness, facilitate the exchange of opinions, and often act as incentives to betterment. At the same time, dialectically as it were, the content of consciousness and opinions tends to become light and the incentives to loose themselves in purely personal advancement and snobbishness. The advantage gained from the larger *area* of contacts in cities is taken away by the still larger *number* of contacts which make for the loosening of solidarity and end in the weakening of civic character. Elsewhere, the 'personality' of a city is sought to be maintained by pride in its history, as in England, or in its present achievements and future possibilities, as in the U.S.A. Municipal

enterprise and public works everywhere form an important agency for fostering civic 'personality'. In India this agency does not work on the Youth. Excepting in Aligarh, which is only a town, no urban municipality is proud of the university within or close to its area, and no university student seems to be conscious of the existence of a municipality, not to speak of an understanding of its role in collecting the fissiparous tendencies created by the storm and stress of urban life. The usual connexion between municipal life and university life is confined to a seat for a teacher-representative on the municipal Board or for a city father on the university-court, and for students to taxes on cycles and cinemas. This is insufficient and tenuous. But the main point is the loss of social solidarity and the rise of ephemeral associations among university students. At present, these latter are grouped on territorial and denominational bases. Punjabis, Kashmiris, Shias, Sunnis, Bengalis and Andhras congregate for two years or so, and they go back without any heightened feeling about India or the U.P., without any fond memory of their Alma Mater, without any understanding of diverse culture-patterns in the country. Partial congregation is natural, but the process of acculturization is also necessary. It is clear that the counter-agencies of heterogeneity are not operating among the Youth in Indian universities. Whatever is operating comes from politics. I wish I could substitute 'national movement' for politics. But I cannot, for the simple reason that the national movement, I mean, its 'sound' thought, has never countenanced Communism or anti-Communism, Hindu chauvinism and anti-Muslim feeling, or any such polarities which divide the Indian Youth today. University students in these four years have conquered urban heterogeneity only by the supreme effort of relief to Bengal, Bihar and Malabar. And all honour to them, because I know the opposition they had to meet. Relief as a means for correcting the evils of urban life posits the permanent need for relief, which, as everybody will admit, is not a happy condition. Be that as it may, the recent relief work has brought the Indian youth some knowledge of rural conditions. Gandhiji's constructive programme pointed the way towards the acquisition of more knowledge, its stabilization and the consequential increase in the sense of social solidarity. It is idle to minimize the difficulties and dangers of such an all-out programme. It runs full tilt against the mighty forces making for urbanization. My own view is that these latter will win in the long run. But it will be unfortunate for India if her young surrender without a stiff fight to the discrete abstractions, the 'casual, superficial and short-lived relations' of urbanized life. In that process of earnest resistance, those very forces will gain in balance.

(4) Another significant feature in the psycho-social attitude of our young men and women at the universities is the gradual displacement of primary, personal contacts by secondary and tertiary impersonal contacts. Contacts with relations and members of the family are still there, but in large cities they are mainly with new friends, mostly temporary ones, and with such impersonal items as newspapers, books, radio and cinema. Leaders', eminent professors' and thinkers' views and voices they hear, but their hands they do not shake. This too is a world-wide phenomenon. Cities are places of exchange of goods; their opportunities of association are large, impermanent and specific, their population is vast and congestion great. But the poignancy of the Indian situation arises from the fact that the transition

from habits formed round the personal relations of family, caste and village community into new impersonal conventions built round novel interests has been sudden. And the consequences have not always been happy. Fear of anonymity and impersonality has led to the exaggeration of certain bonds of student-grouping, like local jealousies, sectarian feeling and ideological conflict—bonds which it is at least the philological duty of universities to remove. If students are merely numbers on the roll, they are no better than employees in a large factory. Personal contacts of teachers with students are, however, no solution of the problem of de-personalization of our Youth caused by urban life. Surely, a teacher cannot lecture honestly for three periods a day, do his own research work and private studies, do even the minimum wire-pulling necessary for his preferment and prestige demanded respectively by increasing family responsibilities and the itching of his undoubted intelligence to have some power, and yet mix with say two to three hundred students who pass through his hands every year. After all, a teacher is also human, and it is the very limitations of his humanity which prevent him from establishing personal contacts with his students. The teacher-student relation is therefore subsidiary to the problem of urbanization when you come to think of it.) Personally, I see no permanent way out of the city's anonymity and the evils in its train which affect the students most. So long as 'public demand' is a condition precedent to the establishment of colleges and universities I cannot be very hopeful. Public demand means public subscriptions; subscriptions can come only from rich people; people become rich only in cities; and why should they be so generous as to subscribe for a university elsewhere? Exceptions like Santiniketan,

Aligarh, Annamalai and Poona only prove the rule. Every nationality cannot be so regardful of higher learning as Maharashtra. And one does not pray for the establishment of a university on any snow-clad peak of the Himalayas just for its cool and clear atmosphere declared to be so necessary for dispassionate, scientific, pure, i. e. non-political attitude towards problems like say Reconstruction of India's Economy. Nor can every student afford to engage efficient tutors to teach him at home in order that his personal relationship may be kept in contact. So, regional universities in non-industrial centres (they should be big towns), appear to be the only solution. It is a temporary solution no doubt, because non-industrial towns will soon become industrial ones. Also, let us not forget that industrial cities confer a few undoubted benefits upon their youthful residents, e. g. alertness of mind, information, up-to-dateness, etc., which India with so much leeway to make can ill afford to neglect. But I think that these benefits can be retained and cultivated, among other means, by a healthy student movement. I say 'student movement', because I have failed to notice any university teachers' movement in my experience of over twenty-two years. The learned conferences, annually held and annually dispersed, are mainly physical movements of delegates. One may occasionally detect a social, even an economic movement there. Many examinerships and offices are 'fixed' by 'human' contacts in these conferences. No, no, we teachers cannot materially contribute to the process of 'personalizing' the Indian Youth by countering the depersonalizing forces acting upon them through the urban life. We can do a little, but not much.

5. THE INDIAN YOUTH AS WARDS OF GUARDIANS

Nearly all sociologists agree that the arrangement of beliefs, attitudes and ideas is largely conditioned by the socio-economic grouping. Without settling the issues of the primary cause, nature *versus* nurture, and such other vexing ones, we may accept the generalization for the present. In any case, it is true for the Indian Youth of today. He or she is essentially a ward of the guardian; and the guardian mostly belongs to the 'middle class', a group which consists mainly of members drawing their income from liberal professions, trade, commerce, and ownership or tenancy of land. This group has a mental pattern of its own, enveloping and motivating the actions of the Young. Due to peculiar circumstances, it has acquired prestige beyond its number. Rightly or wrongly, people associate progress with its fortunes. And so long as the connexion between national regeneration or social change and higher education is thought to be close, an analysis of the make-up of the middle class mind is relevant to the sociological study of the Indian Youth eager to evolve a new order for India.

A few historical remarks are necessary at this stage. The Indian middle class as we find it today has little or no connexion with the middle class of pre-British India. The present middle class or the *bhadralok* is a creation of the European East India Companies in the first instance and then of the British rule. It was recruited at the end of the eighteenth century and the beginning of the nineteenth from the agents, the guarantors, the *mutsuddis*, the banias of the commercial concerns, trading and financial houses of non-Indian origins and interests. Even in the matter of land-ownership (it is questionable whether it was ownership at all) the new landlords were *not* the old landlords except in a few cases. The trading and commercial interests of pre-British days were so completely liquidated that practically no modern magnate of trade and commerce can push back his family's greatness beyond a hundred and fifty years. On the other hand, there are a number of middle-class families whose third or fourth ancestor had profited by western education. In short, the social and economic sterilization of the trading and commercial group—a group which had always been playing a progressive role in Indian culture—coincided with the formation of a middle class that began to acquire land and imbibe western education. The rise of banks and 'houses', the new land and revenue laws, and the spread of western education formed a constellation under whose auspices the new middle class was born. The timing was perfect. It is not to be understood, however, that the new group had no affiliations to the basic social structure, viz. the caste system. The earlier batch of the English educated came from fairly orthodox, upper castes. And yet, the intellectual allegiance to cast rules soon became weak. The first impact nearly severed it, until a reaction came in the wake of nationalism to patch it up. In the absence of Muslims' enthusiasm for English education, the middle class was mostly Hindu in composition. When Sir Syed Ahmad sought to correct the deficiency, the Hindus had stolen a march. Much of the subsequent Hindu-Muslim misunderstanding is traceable to the difference in the time of the start and in the tempo. Such a middle class is not the authentic one that we come across in Victorian England; with limited prospects it could not resemble the bureaucracy in Prussia and Germany; having an agricultural bias of the non-cultivating, ground-rent surplus-enjoying type, it was very different from the class that stabilized the southern and the middle-western States in the U.S.A.; and burdened with a foreign medium of instruction it could not, as a class, rise to its full stature. The Indian middle class did what it could in these circumstances. A graft it was on the social stock, and a graft it has remained ever since, if one looks closely enough.

Indian middle class attitudes partake of the above origin. At their best, they can be described as Liberal. English Liberalism, as is well known, has had at least three strands: (*a*) faith in the individual, (*b*) faith in nationalism, and (*c*) a mixture of philosophical radicalism and utilitarianism. Each was sought to be assimilated by the educated Indian. But being what he was, the process often produced queer results. The first batch of the middle class consisted of individuals who developed their selfhood in conflict with the social taboos and simultaneously in harmony with Victorian ideas of social progress—which they believed was conterminous with the British rule in India, if only it were a little less rigid, a little more sympathetic in the matter of higher appointments. Character could not be identical with the character of Smiles' Self-Help because profit making in business and industry did not get much chance in India *minus* Bombay; but it could be easily measured in terms of titles, jagirs and such other forms of success in life. And yet when one remembers one's grandfather and his friends, admiration for their uphill fight and rise to fortune, their marked character and individuality cannot fail to excite admiration. The only other thing to remember is that these strong Indian individuals were only the shadows of the solid Victorian individuals in England whose intrinsic merit has been so generously recognized and whose self-complacency so brilliantly debunked. If the English Victorians, Gordon and Gladstone, Tennyson and Browning, Huxley and John Stuart Mill had a centre of weakness, the Indian Victorians had a chasm, and feet of clay to boot, not all the clay coming from the Indian soil either. They put up a mask of strength; they wanted to come back to the traditions; but it was a mask; and it was a pathetic attempt at revivalism to fortify self-respect. The course of Indian character had turned askew, and nothing could set it back aright before a fresh inspiration was forthcoming.

It came through nationalism. The Indian middle class had always been nationalistic but in the early stage, nationalism was a timid affair. Between Tilak and Aurobindo, it was lifted on to the vital plane and transformed into nobler stuff. The former kept the 'political' nature of the struggle and tried to base the struggle on certain (for him the Hindu) foundations of Indian culture. Sociologically, Tilak's strength was in retentiveness. But, for the first time, nationalism began to have character in the Victorian sense, i. e. as the gift of self-reliance and resistance, sacrifice for an ideal and absence of fear. Aurobindo stressed all that and more. He constructed a metaphysic of nationalism which was popularized by Bepin Chunder Pal. That metaphysic was further raised into spiritualism until at last India was merged in the cosmos. Aurobindo's contribution to the formation of nationalism may appear thin today, but there was a time when the entire Indian middle class took its cue of patriotism from his writings. A constructive worker like Lala Lajpat Rai drew his sustenance from Aurobindo's philosophy. A whole race of Indian youth was reared by it, a race of men who played with their life for the sake of their motherland. Yet, the middle class attitude could not become a habit Aurobindo, Lal, Bal, Pal were admired; the mother-cult spread; emotions and intellect were stirred; the new band of nationalists became heroes. But the canker could not be removed. The heredity of the Indian middle class triumphed over the achievements of its individual members. At this distance of time, one observes how the resurgent national movement suffered from its structural defects. The Indian middle class admired the terrorists in private and wangled for Government jobs for its wards; it was radical in politics, and conservative and revivalist in social thought and practice; it read classics but behaved like romantics. These contradictions arose from that anarchism which an unrooted group or a band of emigres cannot but cherish as the only remaining agency for restoration. Anarchism as a creed cannot be rooted in history; it is essentially ahistorical, and therefore, it cannot either spring from or create national traditions or character. The dispossessed and the parasite suffer from the feeling of having been cheated by history. This grievous sense of historical wrong without an opportunity of righting it on a national scale accounts for the tangles in the attitudes and the peculiar nature of culture of the Indian middle class. There *is* an undeniable trait of anarchism (which is not merely the *reductio ad absurdum* of a fake individualism) in the make-up of the Indian middle class, the members of which being Indians by birth have sociality bred in their bones. Proofs of the existence of this acquired anarchistic trait can be easily heaped up, but one should suffice. Positively, just as there *is* sympathy for direct action and sabotage, so negatively, there *is* antipathy to Marxism and its historical and social realism among the Indian middle-class. Expression is another story. An English public-school boy would call it sneakish. Social psychologists would put it to frustration which on a wide scale posits an emotional undertone, a subterranean current, dark like Stygian waters and capable of undermining whole layers of law and order. Alas! the pity of it is that it wrecks many a thing besides.

If human nature is full of contradictions, the nature of the Indian middle class dwells in contrarieties. In a sense, Philosophical Radicalism is distinguishable from Utilitarianism; in another context, both are offshoots of a trunk of ideas which grew out of a social economy that had been changing over from the division of labour in handicrafts into one of differentiation of functions in machinofacture, in short, from the production of goods for consumption into the production of commodities for profit by exchange. The swing-over atomized the old society into individual units each competing with the other. Its ideology was a composite pattern which left its impress upon the Indian educated. The hedonistic calculus or the moral arithmetic, the mistrust of obligations and the consequent stress upon rights, and individual rights at that, the dominance of egoistic motives and their automatic equation to social good, the grounding of group-interests upon economic ones, and above all, the charging of worldly conduct with the spirit of competition between one individual and another *and* of the spiritual atmosphere with a belief in ultimate harmony and progress—these and many more traits are observable in the code of the Indian middle class. They collaborated here as elsewhere in the formation of national sentiment. The Liberal-Utilitarian radical of England was a great patron of the national movement in Europe because he believed in the right of nations, for him equal to individuals, to live without let or hindrance. If he did not realize the implications of free trade with poor, struggling nations, it was not his fault. Similarly, the Indian Liberal Radical (he would not like to be named a Utilitarian, although he was one) was a patron of the National Congress, and if he was not always alive to the rights of women, the Depressed Classes and of Muslims, he could not be blamed for conscious hypocrisy. What added to the confusion, however, was a big dose of Mazzini. The latter's emphasis on Duty corrected the pleasure-aspect of hedonism and implanted a religious fervour into the heart of Indian nationalism. Surendranath Bannerjee was deeply influenced by Mazzini although he was not a religious man. People may not detect the presence of hedonism and moral arithmetic in our national conduct today. But it has only gone under. Just as Calvinism was partly responsible for the rational outlook and ethic of European capitalism, the peculiar adaptation of British Utilitarianism has been at work behind the emergence of the economic being in India. His rational, protestant ethic, with a dash of revivalism *a la* Mazzini, is latent among the Government servants and patent among the Indian capitalists of today. Their account with British Imperialism is entered in a sort of moral double keeping. It is all very complicated, but complication is the heart of all tragedy. If it is also at the root of comedy, well, the Indian middle class is a bit comic, isn't it? (Not to be quoted by Beverely Nichols. How does one spell that name?)

Such is the mental make-up of the guardians of the Indian student community. It is in this climate that the Indian youth has to work and live. As such, he is not a full-fledged youth, only a ward of his guardian, a tragi-comic being.

The Indian youth has imbibed all the strength and weakness of his guardian's attitudes hardened in these hundred years If the necessary adjustments have not been as fruitful as one expected, the credit is mainly the guardian's. For, it is the guardian, and not the ward, who sets the norm of the ward's life. But while the norm continues to be justified by the guardian on the strength and as an evidence of character, the conditions for reaching the norm have ceased to exist. Thus for example, the guardian's individualism has been found to be inadequate by the ward for whom the immediate prospects measured in terms of safe berths and respectable wages are dark. Consequently, the 'world' seems to the young to be much less elastic and resilient to the pressure of 'character'. As a corollary, there is a general lamentation by the guardians over the loss of character among this generation. A sociologist may argue, however, that this character was not much of a character but a mask in imitation of the face of the master race for the main object of getting on, and therefore, its disappearance is not a serious loss to the nation. At the same time, one must point out (*a*) that individualism had placed a premium upon certain moral traits which, however narrow they might have been, stood in good stead when the older values were being disintegrated, and (*b*) that their liquidation creates a void so long as newer values are not thrown up and do not crystallize the conduct of the young. 'Individualism is dead; and long live individualism' cannot be proclaimed.

In this interregnum reign fear and confusion. Nature abhors a vacuum, but chaos loves it. And we see fear possessing the soul of the Indian youth who must needs submerge himself in a party, abdicate his intelligence on behalf of a leader dictator, extinguish himself like a devotee before his *guru*, and stun all stirrings of his brain by the blow of his 'ideology'. The Indian youth is afraid of loneliness. It is an epidemic of agoraphobia that has seized the mind of our young people making them feel like old maids nervous at passing open spaces and cross-roads and feeling secure in their little corners counting beads, mumbling names of saints and dead relations in the same breath.

The difficulties of the Indian youth are not to be minimized. In the absence of older values and with the uncertain, undefined and strange nature of the emerging ones the gaping void has to be closed, and closed by the young themselves. The middle class guardians are not going to be of any help. On the contrary, they are determined to oppose the formation of new values. Already the message has gone round that there is ample room for 'free enterprise', i. e. stark individualism, within the ambit of planning, i. e. State-control. Already, the distrust of the Soviet experiment has infected the intelligentsia who have discovered that Soviet bureaucracy has finished off the individual. Already, the Indian *bourgeoisie* is on the march, and the whole texture of its argument is individualistic. Indian intellectuals have already swelled the chorus, and the notable ones among them—those who are blessed by official and non-official patronage and have thereby acquired prestige in the eyes of the guardians—are notable and influential on account of their ability to show the limitations of planned socialist thought and practice. Books by Max Eastman, Burnham, Hayek have become the pabulum of the Indian educated; Sir Theodore Gregory rules Delhi thought; Socialism is being re-considered; and the Gandhian plan is being mooted as an alternative to planning on the basis of non-individualistic, non-competitive principles. Soviet planning may or may not have been a success; the Gandhian plan may or may not be typically Indian or adequate for India's needs; Socialism may or may not stand in need of being re-considered; what is important is the fact that all this mock-ferment tends to mislead the young men of India by staging on the sly a come-back for individualism in reaction to any step beyond it. Sociologically, it is a throw-back, because in the present disposition of social forces reaction is natural, and what is natural is hostile to the deliberate creation of new values, aye, of culture which is a matter of joint human artifice and social engineering. For the guardians, who have been bred in Anglo-Saxon individualism and liberalism and who trace their own success, and flatter themselves on it, to their self-help or 'character', the new cult of the individual, even if no longer of the rugged one but only the common man type, is going to be still more natural, i. e. moral; and for the wards, viz. the youth and the students, it bids fair to be the source of their chief difficulty and the main fetter of their spiritual enslavement. If the youth are more than mere wards, if they are really young, they had better take care of this cult right from now; otherwise they will be swamped by the social philosophy of the technical personnel or the managerial class either of whom is only the old middle class rendered a little more competent and aggressive by the change of masters and of situation.

We have noted how the Indian middle class has always been nationalistic in a way. Since the advent of Gandhiji in Indian politics, the quality of Indian nationalism has undergone a change., It is no longer a legal career punctuated by politics ; it is a serious business demanding the whole of a man. The preceding movement was also deadly serious, and it had demanded death. But death it was, not life So, a younger generation flocked under Gandhiji's banner and gave its best to the country at his call. Political conduct now became a moral issue, with this difference that while the ethic of anarchist terrorism was dominated by the death instinct of individual heroes, that of the non-co-operation movement had behind its constructive programme the urges of living of a large mass of people. True that the earlier movement was more dramatic, and therefore more interesting than the latter ; true also that the former had launched a number of big schemes ; but the latter movement had more traffic with the people in being more conscious of their needs and more solicitous of their welfare. Indian youth could now canalize their hatred and frustration into some channel flowing out of the urban areas and classes into the countryside. It was a partial compensation. When the Civil Disobedience movement was started, the Indian youth discovered new content in nationalism. Jail lost its terror, and the middle class guardian was privately proud of his ward's moral courage—a positive gain on both sides. The no-rent campaign, reported to have been precipitated by Pandit Jawaharlal, introduced history into the ethics of Indian politics. The Indian youth remained loyal to Gandhiji and improved their own morals by the leader's precept and example, but the religious element involved in any process of call and response was modified by a form, albeit a vague one, of historical and economic understanding of the social and political forces. The change from a Britisher (the White Devil he had once been called) to British Imperialism as the object of opposition blunted the edge of personal feeling and hatred; the popularity of Socialism at this juncture toned down the religious colour in the ethico-political ensemble; and the burning sincerity and the majestic courage of the new hero, Jawaharlal, was ready to do the rest. For the time, the intransigent Jawaharlal, the socialist, non-religious Jawaharlal, carried the day, and the Indian youth's life was charged with new meaning. The Indian youth movement, as we know it today, is Jawaharlal's affair. Later on, his recurring eventual surrenders to Gandhiji's conclusions created some confusion. If Moscow has displaced Wardha in the mind of a number of young people, it is at least partly due to Panditji's split personality. The future of the Indian youth in the next few years is going to depend in an appreciable manner upon the attitude he will take towards the Indian Communists. A bigger issue is the still newer significance of nationalism which the Indian young men and women are willing to create and which can be more easily created with Jawaharlal's assistance than with anybody else's among India's leaders.

What exactly is this fresh significance of nationalism which the Indian youth seeks? In spite of its existing high quality, Indian nationalism has betrayed a few deficiencies. Probably, the Indian youth is only vaguely aware of them. But they are there in the region of the sub-conscious. The deficiencies in our nationalism arise from the fact that the desire for political advance is ahead of India's actual economic and social changes. This lag is best seen in the structure of middle class life. The middle class family-structure is still mainly feudal in the domination of the *karta* or the patriarch over the younger members; and in the upper strata, it is that of the *bourgeois*-individualistic-romantic type in the limited freedom of choice given to wards in marriage and occupation. It is also mainly governed by caste considerations in so far as patronage in service and business goes to the members of the same caste by preference. (The competitive system is still an exception.) The guardian and the candidate expect patronage from 'the brethren'. Changes in family-life, in the status of women, in the village economy, caste system, etc. have no doubt occurred, but their rate is much slower than what the youth thinks should happen in the political sphere. Communism, even Socialism, is not an exact reflection of the changing objective situation in India, and yet a vast majority of young persons want it. This has introduced a note of unreality into our nationalism. It could not be helped. What the Indian youth greatly wants is to remove this unreality. And it has been sought to be done in two ways (*a*) through the kisan-mazdoor movement and (*b*) by the linking up of India's destiny with the world's progressive forces. The former had not yielded the expected result because the rate of Indian industrialization, in spite of the war, has been really slow; and the latter attempt seems to have fallen between two stools, hatred of British Imperialism and an uncritical appreciation of the Soviet achievement. We notice the consequence of the latter in the policy of exclusion of Communists from Congress ranks and the campaign of their vilification. Even if we attributed it to the confusion among the elders and their bankruptcy of statesmanship and noticed its resemblance to Jew-baiting, even if we put it to the springs of the ego which must defend its own weakness by palming it off on a scape-goat, we would still be driven by the sociology of the situation to conclude that the effort of the youth to create new meaning for nationalism has not yet bridged the gulf between the reality of the social and economic process and the ideal of a government planned on principles of full democracy and social good. Thus it is that even the advanced sections of the youth still remain unrealistic. But it is not the unrealism of the usual type in which a young person marries the guardian's choice in all filial piety, practises all the revered customs of old and otherwise betrays all the attitudes of earlier centuries, and yet vaguely wants self-determination for India as a political unit. The unreality of the Communist youth, to take the extreme section, comes from an overweening optimism, a blind faith in History incarnated in Stalin's good wishes and capacity. Consciousness of historical forces is an advance, but optimism and blind faith are no substitutes for the reality of planned creation. The guardians come in here to increase the gulf and enhance the unreality. They are merely anti-British political beings still secretly wanting their wards to become I.C.S., Deputy-Collectors and the like. In this family-atmosphere of the Indian youth, his nationalism is a marvel of self-help, clear thinking and honesty. It is a sight for the gods to see fathers coaching their sons and mothers blessing them with sacred grass and ointment on the day of the interview with public service commissions. Mofussil lawyers behave with more dignity before the judges than what the guardians prescribe for their wards.

The second deficiency in the Indian nationalism has been the neglect of the possibilities of vast sections of the Indian people to enrich the quality of Indian nationalism in their own way. At first, Indian political Leaders wanted to exclude; now they tolerate. It is only very recently that the contribution of whole groups of people is being recognized. Recognition is yet half-hearted, non-intellectual, politically expedient. But that is the way in which recognition proceeds among those who have been enslaved by Anglo-Saxon modes of consciousness. The stages of the reactions of the British mind to a novelty have been thus tabulated : Non-recognition, enmity and opposition, eccentric acceptance, and lastly 'I told you so', 'I knew it before', we did it long ago'. Later historians of the Indian national movement will no doubt discover the leaders' solicitude for the kisan mazdoor, for the so-called Depressed Classes, for the Muslim community in the texts of old resolutions. For the present, however, orthodox Indian nationalism is not fully conscious of two historical facts, viz: (*a*) that there are at least two major classes within a nation, and (*b*) that there must needs be a number of nationalities to make up a nation. It is to the credit of certain sections of the Indian youth that these two facts are being brought forward to the notice of our leaders. Gandhiji's acceptance of Muslim claims shows his flexibility, but as yet, all talk of proletariat and Pakistan remains for the middle class guardians outside nationalism and inside the first three stages of recognition mentioned before. To put it frankly, the guardian's attitude towards the dynamic of nationalism offered by class-conflict and the renaissance of the nationalities is one of sullen opposition. For him, the chamar is just an untouchable, the Muslims are a menace, and the mazdoor-kisan is always a servant to be pitied and patronized during good behaviour. No guardian seems to be aware that the so-called Depressed Classes and the Muslims are the economic have-nots and the social protestants in the history of Indian culture. The Indian youth, therefore, wants a different significance and a different dynamic of nationalism.

It is not easy to suggest a way out of this impasse. Wholesale massacre of guardians being ruled out as unpractical, illegal, immoral and uneconomic, moral pressure is worthy of attempt. For example, the young man may refuse to offer for his examination subjects recommended by his guardian for their fetching-value; he may refuse to take up the double course, M.A. and LL.B., in two years; he may refuse to marry before he earns well; on marriage he may offer to start a family of his own; he may infect his little brothers and sisters with his ideas. (Read Bukanin's life for this technique of resistance, if you hate Communism and Karl Marx.) In other countries, however, moral pressure is not considered sufficient by the young. But the Indian middle class is a highly moral race, and it is only sound tactics to adopt the means of your enemy even for another end. If moral pressure fails, then Socialism is the only way. It is a desperate remedy, but the disease is fatal. Socialism will no doubt expose the Indian guardian's feet of clay and destroy much of the India he thinks he knows. But it may build up a new set of guardians by catching them young. After all, guardianship is not finished in a day. It runs through generations, and if this generation of the youth keeps up its intellectual honesty, the guardian-ward relationship of the next generation need not be the same as it is.

Teachers are no good in this matter of changing the guardian-ward axis, and for obvious reasons. They themselves are guardians of their wards; they themselves are the derelict of the Indian middle class concentrating all its vices and its outmoded ideologies, individualism, sneaking nationalism, confused radicalism and all the rest of it. What is worse is teachers' gift of rationalization and quotation. And they are very disinterested by virtue of their intellectualism. In fact, teachers don't exist in this country—they are looked upon by the guardian as guardian-tutors of their wards. And so do the wards who want to do well at examinations. When the wards are four to five hundred a year and success means a first-class by mugging up notes, the teacher-tutor is helpless.

It seems that the sociology of Indian youth points towards a cross-road of moral pressure and historical understanding. It is a cross-road where the Indian youth stands facing the sun lured by vistas opened in the dawn. May a sociologist hope that no unkempt grave of a suicide disfigure the cross-road to be cursed by the passerby!

6. THE TEACHER-STUDENT NEXUS

I wonder if it is realized by all concerned that teachers in high schools, colleges and universities can be of very limited use in the solution of the problems of Indian youth. The general idea seems to be that the teachers have the sole or the mojor responsibility in this regard. A small dose of realism, however, can expose its absurdity. The social unit is still the family, and as I have often pointed out, it is the middle-class family, and no teacher-student axis can break it, whatever might have been the situation in good old days when *gurus* could 'catch 'em young'. If the period of contact between the two parties could have been longer than what it is—which is seldom more than two years at the outside and that also made up of one or two hours a day with other teachers' influence competing—then probably the chances of conditioning would have been better. I wonder if the public really knows the class routines. Anything from four to six subjects are taught a day in schools and colleges; each class runs to at least fifty boys on the average; in some private colleges as many as two hundred boys are on the roll with half attending; lectures are for fifty minutes; when the bell goes, a long sigh of relief is heaved, by masters and pupils alike; and school and college hours begin from 10-30 (wartime) and go up to past four. In these circumstances, the only contact between masters and pupils can be of a theosophical nature. The story is yet incomplete. Private tuitions must be undertaken to supplement the income which not unoften is a few rupees less than the official amount. School teachers in certain institutions have not been able to secure even that miserable dole of dearness allowance which the officially described menials' have got. Probably, the most pitiable creatures in this land of ours today are the teachers and their women-folk. Add to it the glorious tradition of joint-family and the highly moral ignorance of birth control, and the teacher's responsibility to discharge any capital responsibility becomes thin indeed. It pains one to write it; but the presumption beneath that general idea of human contact etc. is that teachers should *not* be human, that they must *not* be family-men, that they must be anti-social, that they shall have no appetites lest these call for satisfaction in the way of a change in the summer vacation, purchase of books and the like, and that they should be beggar-devotees to the cause of education. An ideal true to type, no doubt, but the difficulty is that non-human creatures like ascetics are not always the fittest agency for humanization—which is the active principle of influencing young minds and the real strength of any social nexus.

Besides, can any teacher, on his own account, unwind the threads of the mental pattern that has been woven round the life of a middle class youth? Let us take concrete cases. The ideal student is one who prepares all the possible questions in order to get a first; the best teacher is one who satisfies that desire by 'points' spoken slowly or dictated. A little enquiry reveals that such a method is inevitable in a context where not merely a degree but a *good* position, now that there is keen competition, is the *only* passport to jobs, unless, of course, the relations intervene. Most students have no patrons; and so they must fall back upon gold medals and resounding testimonials. Students, so long as they are natural students, i.e. when they are not mugging up to score at the examination, do not eat their hearts out for jobs. They do when they realize that they are responsible wards of their guardians.

I make haste to assert that restriction of the number of students is no solution at all. It is a thoroughly unsocial, and hence a mischievous suggestion. Aptitude, however, is a different matter. And there too, the teacher is ineffective. For one, if he had any special aptitude, he would have been elsewhere; for another, and this is an important point, no special aptitude discovered by Western psychologists and their Indian imitators or what is demanded by the educational planners, official or otherwise, fits in with the *concrete social situation* as we find it reflected upon the student mind. Musical aptitude? How many guardians would gladly send their wards to music schools in response to the urge of the musical aptitude? Is music a paying proposition? What happens to the musical maids a year after they get married? Their new relations talk about laryngitis. Painting, sculpture, architecture, each is alleged to have a corresponding aptitude. Is that related to the Indian middle-class life? Technical aptitudes so far never got a chance. I hear that they will get it soon. But then the middle-class respectability will have gone, and the structure will have collapsed. The ability so long groomed has been that of quill-driving, and so it remains the only noticeable aptitude. That is exactly what many of the faculties have actually been reduced to by our education.

Can, any educational institution that we know be useful in changing this educational system? That will be hara-kiri. Once more, let us be realistic. A non-official institution is a capitalistic concern; it is usually started for profit, run for profit and carried on on 'business principles' to show a surplus for which, teachers' wages must be low and the number of students paying fees large. When the endowment is of a private philanthropist or a group, the motive of profit is replaced by benevolent despotism. It is not simply in Japanese schools that teachers are not allowed to breathe 'dangerous thoughts' (one hopes that things are better in U.S.A. since the days of E. A. Ross' and Harold Laski's relief from duty.) But the hold of Indian philanthropists upon the teachers of their institutions is a strangle-hold rendered doubly dangerous by its very invisibility. To what extent even the highest educational institutions are run on principles of business-economy can be seen by all who care. Heads of departments must have the largest number of boys; positively third-rate students should be allowed to take the Honours course; plucked boys must have special classes; diplomas and degrees have to be given in the minimum number of years; double-course in two years must be permitted: questions should be easy and the percentage of passes high—and all for ensuing quantity which means profit, surplus, income *minus* expenditure larger than in any previous year. I repeat, quantity is not the villain of the piece; it is the 'business-principle'. Can any educational institution run on 'business-lines' ever change the social context of which it is a reflection and undertake to impart education for a completely different order? So far as I know, education in civilized countries is a spending concern, and not a saving one. The latest report indicates that even in Great Britain, a country inhabited by people with almost a congenital mistrust of knowledge and knowledgeable men, of theories and theorists, a people with its ethos planted in instincts rather than in reason, a people whose serpent (*kundalini*) coils itself round the anus (*muladhar*) rather than in the centre of the brain (*sahasrar*,) to use *tantrik* analogies in these days of power-politics, a country whose Government axes teachers salaries in its economy-drive and has been uniformly niggardly in fostering research, a country again which in spite of all that and in pursuance of non-educational considerations had offered through its metropolitan university the model of the Calcutta University, the prototype of nearly all Indian universities—I say, even that country and that people is proposing to raise teachers' salaries to the grade enjoyed by civil servants. It is not suggested that Indian teachers should be placed on the footing of civil servants. They, I mean, the Indian members there of, even when they play the lord in their districts, are often ashamed of the part they have to play, and they cover their shame in diverse ways. Theirs is *not* an enviable lot *pace* their salaries and wages. Nobody wants teachers to be dissociated beings like the Imperial or the provincial servants. What is pleaded is that so long as influence is a function of status, and status is that of money, that so long as some contact with books and ideas enables the teacher to acquire the freshness of mind that attracts pupils and makes lectures and talks interesting, and further that in so far as easy circumstances make for the normal human integrity of the teacher's behaviour towards men and things, this exploitation of educated men by the public and educational authorities and institutions must cease. To argue that some teachers will get lazy with increments in wages is of the same order of reasoning as that of the employer who would keep the wages of his employees low lest they take to toddy.

My purpose is not to air the grievances of teachers as such. They come in to prove the worthlessness of the opinion that the teacher-student relation is a social one. Exceptions must be there, logically. Actually, however, I have yet to see any considerable number of teachers who are more interested in their work, which includes the welfare of students, than in their economic uplift. Otherwise why should there be so much of politics in educational centres? It is sheer nonsense to blame the materialistic civilization that revolves round money. Money has come to stay. It is not money, but its distribution that is wrong. Subordinate service grade one, grade two; provincial, service grade one and grade two; lecturers grade one, grade two; readers who are heads and not heads of departments; professors senior and junior; these Byzantine divisions would have been envied by Raghunath Shiromani. This is not caste, but classification with a vengeance. Thus have the teachers been converted into the *bourgeoisie*, and the *bourgeoisie* split into the large and the petty. No wonder that teachers often betray a sneaking fondness for dictators in the name of discipline. Listen to their talk about the decay in youthful morals and the dire need of 'leaders' and 'strong men'. Only, they forget they are the weaklings. All that I say is that the public who know these things should occasionally remember that teachers have been made weaklings by the very social process which holds the same public in its grip and which that public still chooses to consider to be eternal and sacrosanct. In this vicious cycle nobody can be of any good to anybody.

Shall we then despair? A little can yet be done by the teacher to influence youth. The governing principle of the deed emanates not so much from the usual moral considerations or any philosophy of individualism as from the main features of the context. It is nothing less and nothing more than the abolition of the barriers between one segment of knowledge and another, on the one hand, and between knowledge and life on the other, by the supreme strategy of historical and sociological understanding of the whole process in terms of its contradictions and crises. On this and this alone can the teacher proceed to discharge his social responsibilities towards the problems of youth in general and of the Indian Youth in particular. Beyond this is the region of sentimental idealism.

The cardinal fact about the social situation is that it is changing. No longer do the old values by themselves possess any creative competence; but new values are still inchoate, and they still are insufficient substitutes for the old. A changing order demands a dynamic approach and a flexible, experimental temper rather than the fixedness of a definite world-view. In other words, social reality is now to be realized as a process, and not to be taken as a category. Flexibility connotes choice, which in its turn demands knowledge of the field in its entirety.

Experimental temper suggests the spirit of adventure. Here the teacher's function begins. His part is not moral in the traditional sense, because morality is social, and that society which lent morality to the *guru-sishya* relation of old is gone; his part is intellectual, because the brain is the seat of all trends, and it is all the trends that must be apprehended and given their dues and latitudes in the supreme adventure of the collective creative spirit, viz. the deliberate creation of yet another Indian Renaissance. The teacher's knowledge must therefore aim at covering the whole arena of human intellect.

It is not such an impossibility as people imagine. Just as modern military strategy continually seeks for the weakest points of the enemy to overwhelm his resistance by local superiority and then sidethrusts for rolling out in order to cover the wide area behind, thereby assuring the independence of local actions within the ambit of the master-plan, so the modern fight against ignorance can yield the best results by discovering the crises in each branch of knowledge, using them as thrust-points, and then spreading out on all sides according to the social directives of living. The first thing to do is to discover the crises and the weakest links and then to blitz away with the massed knowledge. What frightens a scholar is the *amount* of knowledge, its *front* and *surface*, whereas that which should excite his ardour is the feeling of the *crises* in knowledge and the *area* and *depth* of ignorance. So the competent teacher must be perpetually waging a fight against ignorance. This is not dry-as-dust intellectualism. The effective teacher, just because he is more than a specialist in virtue of his adventurous ability to relate the parts of knowledge to the history and wholeness of knowledge through his sense of crisis in human affairs, simultaneously discharges his duty of humanizing the teacher-student relation. When competence and human effectiveness meet in the same person, the social function has been performed. We are of course referring to collective and not solo efforts.

Historically, this specialization' has been the intellectual counterpart of the 'division of labour' which is reputed to have been brought about in the industrial production of Europe about a century ago through the mechanical inventions that had come to England a few decades earlier. It is also well known how the sciences directly helped the industries to start with an advantage in that era of peace and competition, and thus indirectly assisted the new State, influenced as it already was by the *bourgeoisie*, to overcome the feudal limitations and to pursue its policy of non-interference in the life, liberty and property of its citizens. This policy in actual practice meant the liberty of the *bourgeoisie* to exploit the less fortunate ones. With a stabilized government and an expanding economy, the sciences became Science enjoying the prestige of isolated superiority of the laboratory. Competition eventually became monopoly, but it did not liquidate its competitiveness. So the separation was effected between Science and the sciences, between theorists and practitioners, between men of the laboratories and men tending the machines. In this war, because the economy has been restricted within the borders of a State and the State is in jeopardy, that separation has been abolished with the result that men of pure Science have become men of the applied sciences. And for aught we know, this condition is going to survive the war in Europe and America where the industrial struggle is likely to be waged with a more nervous intensity and on a higher level. But for the time being we will leave aside the future incidence of such a state of affairs upon India.

Now, it has been held—and very rightly too—that the Indian system of production and modes of living are extremely crude; and that, consequent upon the likeness of Indian conditions to those of England, Europe and the U.S.A. in the first part of the nineteenth century, specialization is the first requisite for uplifting the Indian level—which is not quite the right conclusion. Let us be clear on this question of likeness, analogy, model and the like. The point to be firmly held is the *socially necessary* production. To what extent is 'specialization' conducive to that social necessity? In Europe, the trick was done by 'division of labour'. But that 'division' was really and truly a *combination, a co-ordination of multiplied functions*, i.e. a socializing process. It was not, however, allowed to divulge its nature, because that would have involved elimination of profit or its division and sharing with others. And so, 'division of labour' was allowed to remain as just the consequence of mechanical inventions; and its further analysis into the exploitation of technology (and therefore, of the technical experts and specialists) in the interest of industrial profit was not pursued. So the relevant question is this—does India want a repetition of that Smithian division of labour by which the division of society into owners and earners was rationalized into a natural law, a constituent of universal harmony? If the answer is in the affirmative, then let us have specialization of knowledge to help profit swell and wages dwindle in proportion. Otherwise, specialization should not mean anything more than detailed knowledge in relation to living, in short, vocational training. Any education that cuts off vocation from the dynamically integral living is mere technical education—a device exploitable by certain interests. A visit to a laboratory attached to a big firm can easily confirm this view. But it will not, if the mind has been already mystified by that obnoxious and mischievous doctrine of managerial revolution—a variant of technocracy—which has deceived certain sections of the black-coated, white-collared gentry among the employees into believing that they are somebody in the chain of production. Specialists, technicians, the higher personnel are only the respectable among the exploited. In all moments of crisis, at every turn of the social conflict, they go over to the right side. For heaven's sake, therefore, let us understand the social implications of 'specialization', at this stage of India's economic and social development. The relating of knowledge to the concrete social situation of living is the only acceptable social significance of 'specialization'. It is a thousand pities that many Indian intellectuals and young men and women have missed it. The above should not be taken as an argument against industrialization, advancement of knowledge and vocational training.

If all that be true—and here one feels like addressing those who have not yet been taken in—then a teacher, honest to himself, cannot cabin himself within the narrow walls of his special subject and remain an expert but an anti-social being. If honesty be rare, up-to-dateness is in fashion and partriotism is in galore. In progressive countries, there is an important movement towards the Unity of Sciences, Philosophy of the Sciences, etc. First class journals are being published to preach the utter need of a synthesis of the sciences and expound their social functions. It may be that there the immediate impulse as yet is primarily an emotional reaction against the aridity of specialization; very probably, it reflects the marked tendency towards economic amalgamation, international cartels and the One-World-Idea. But the 'pure' intellectual, the 'specialist,' need not know it. It will be sufficient for him to know as an Indian that our traditions have been towards synthesis; that even if these do not live now, there is their memory; that in case the memory too has faded, the very commonly expressed desire that a new India should emerge demands a synthesis of knowledge through an understanding of the crisis in each branch thereof. And synthesis has been the main characteristic of all critical periods, known as Renaissance, in the history of Europe, China and India. Biographies of leaders of Renaissance demonstrate it. These men would synthesize Plato and Aristotle with Christianity, Hindu Upanishads with Islamic faith, Confucianism with Buddhism; they were encyclopaedic men specializing, if at all, in omniscience. A flower does not blossom petal by petal. When the spirit urges, it must seize all or none.

Some will say that those encyclopaedic men, and women too, could take it all in their stride because for them knowledge was strung by Faith: Shakespeare's knowledge of botany and nautical science was held by the remnants of his belief in the angelic hierarchy and in the chain that linked Heaven with Earth: A Madhusudan Saraswaty believed in Brahma and the Vedas: A Sir Brojendra Nath Seal, the last of the giant race of savants, was a man of faith: We can no longer believe, and so, our task of synthesis is difficult. True. But, probably, we the intellectuals, the specialists and the technicians and the managerial class may find it easy to cultivate another set of beliefs centering in the emergence of a new India, an India which is no longer an annexe of the West, an India which does not imitate and flourish on values that sprang out of the culture of one corner of the globe a hundred years ago, but an India that will decide her own destiny and simultaneously seek alliance with the progressive forces in the changing world on the strength of her decision, an India again that will create and create in all the plenitude of her released energies to make amends for the barrenness of those long-drawn years and once more take the lead of the world as she is so eminently fitted to do. This is not the Creative Evolution of Bergson, but a much more fundamental urge, the Creative Unity of Tagore.

Obviously, it is neither the usual intellectualism nor the usual patriotism. It is a manifestation of the very principle of Life itself.

It comes to this then: Specialized knowledge is uninteresting to the young because it is unrelated to the history of knowledge which in its turn is abstracted, divorced from the knowledge of the processes of living. Our forefathers called that integral knowledge *bignan* or 'science'. We are not entitled to confuse it with the science as it is taught in schools and colleges. I call the new synthetic science Sociology; others may call it History. Comte equated the two, and he was probably right. Whichever the modern proper name, the essential point to remember is to relate a specialized knowledge to knowledge, and knowledge to life as it is evolving. If a 'specialist' can do it, he can influence the young; otherwise, he is the neo-barbarian of the age. Students, on their side, should demand the knowledge of that basic relation between knowledge, history and living from their teachers. This, in my view, is the only way of looking at the teacher-student exchange today. When all values are in the melting-pot, character and all that are subordinate to the discovery of the connexion between knowledge and living as a social process. Let us not forget that the root-meaning of the word 'crisis' is judgement. I plead for a critique of knowledge and life as the only possible bond of social union between teachers and students at this crisis of our culture.

7. WHAT TO READ—A FEW PRINCIPLES OF SELECTION

People have noted signs of grief in my views on the problems of Indian Youth. The charge is true. But it has been very difficult for me to avoid sadness. I have been a student all along my life, and my profession as a University teacher brings me into close contact with the best of the young and at their most formative period of life. I also belong to the so-called Indian middle class, a section that once performed certain important duties in spite of handicaps, but which today hardly knows which side of the fence to jump. In fact, however, there are only two sides, one ahead and another behind, unless one chooses to call the metaphysical heaven a third and the materialist mire a fourth. Either the middle class goes ahead and becomes one with the mass by sympathy and action, or it just slides down to its own prejudices and privileges. The sides are not those of the Yogi and the Commissar, the stage-mystic and the stage-communist; they are of the organic, socialized person and the fragmented, atomized individual. Under the existing order, no being born of woman can become a person; at best, he can achieve individuality which is nothing more than a configuration of certain traits and complexes developed in the course of perpetual conflict. It is a conflict of low order, because it is forced upon the human unit in so far as the unit is an isolated unit. It is not the conflict that is necessary for the attainment of higher reaches of humanity and its extension to wider circles. It is just the creakings of mechanical adjustments. The sides, therefore, are conditioned by the problem, viz. how to become a person in the midst of influences that keep a man bound to his struggling, success-hunting, merely-adjusting individuality. Once, we get that clear, the desired direction stands out of the melee. The middle class, in the very interest of its components, must socialize itself. It must liquidate itself, consciously and imaginatively, that is to say, historically. The middle-class youth has a fund of imagination and some will. What he lacks is consciousness. He could have borrowed it from his teachers; but they are busy otherwise. Let him therefore imbibe the historical spirit by his own efforts. A few leaders may help in this supreme intellectual effort; the majority's contribution is to the emotional background. That is very valuable, because consciousness is not an analytical exercise. But caution is necessary lest the emotional contribution kills itself by its own indulgence. Thus I would ask the middle-class Indian Youth to know by his own efforts that his class must merge its interests into those of the mass. The efforts, so far as students *qua* students are concerned, are primarily intellectual, and secondly activist. Truly speaking, theoretical training cannot be separated from practical training. At the same time, emphasis has to be distributed to secure the best results.

In that way, the first question is what to study? Text-books of course, comes the stock answer. But most of the text-books are worthless. They are terribly boring; they are unrelated to India; they avoid the fundamentals and are superficially explicatory. Their analysis is not clarifying, but classifying. They usually make assumptions favouring the *status quo* in practice. People do not know what they are talking when they condemn Socialist literature, Socialist economics, Socialist politics as propagandist. The so-called classics are saturated with ideologies, and dated ones at that. Only, these are cleverly hidden under the guise of natural laws, universal values, and so on. Reactionary ideas may remain implicit in a most innocuous mathematical equation. Exceptions there are even to text-books; but as a general rule they should be used to get through to secure good marks, in short, to fool the examiner, which is an important scholarly pursuit in the nature of things. Text-books are necessary evils. Therefore, it is better to concentrate on one classic in each subject, if any classic is included at all in the curriculum. I know of cases where it is not. Three months' occupation with text-books can do miracles at the examinations; the remaining period out of every two years may be used for study.

'Outside' books, as they are unhappily described, are more important. And it is the duty of the teachers in schools, colleges, and universities, and of civic and rural institutions to provide them, and to guide the young through them. Our libraries are hopelessly inadequate, and probably, there are many towns where the total number of books does not come to the total population number. A book per head is a dream. Probably, when the heaven will fall we will catch the fowls. Meanwhile, let us concentrate on the urban student community. They often look at printed pages. But which to touch? Shall one read them as they come, or shall one discriminate? A few observations may now be made on the principles of selection. They come out of my experience. You may accept them or reject them. But please consider them, as I too have fumbled like every one of you.

If one studies the behaviour of young people towards knowledge, one finds a rythm of interest. It is both wider and deeper than the recurrent stimuli and responses, being more like the periodicity in the sphere of sex. Probably, the two are somehow connected. In any case, the selection of books will have to correspond with the rhythm of interests. Up till ten or twelve, boys and girls, with some difference between themselves, seek the fulfilment of their growing personality in fantasies and imaginative exercises. Then comes the period when the personality seeks to grow on all sides and yet desires to be fixed, shaped and outlined. This stage usually tallies with adolescence. But in India before the storms of adolescence brew the ship is gathered into port. Indian society—and here it is as wise as any primitive tribe in New Guinea—has socialized the storm and the stress phase. In Europe it is a critical one for the individual. There the young man or woman suffers from all manner of agony, religious, sexual, and what not. Mostly, it is romantic agony. Some poetry, some epistles and diaries some sharpening of the edge has come out of it, but penalty too has been paid in suffering and dissolution. Without being enthusiastic about our social order, its tackling of personality during adolescence can be given its dues. Now, given that situation, and it is a situation in which the dogs did not bark, Dr Watson, the difficulties of fixing the personality in the second sweep of the rhythm should be less. And here, the self-educating youth must needs find books purveying accurate information. Scientific literature, history, geography, travels, anthropology and the like correspond to the need of personality to be formed in sharper outline. The subject is immaterial; what is material is more order, more clarity, some edge and accuracy of the shape of personality to come. There is a third movement growing out of the second. In this the need is for yet greater precision of the outline and a simultaneous filling of it, by mass or content of still more information. Precision is achievable by craftsmanship, which is truly speaking the logic of the hand, and by such disciplines as centre in reasoning, induction, deduction, inference, and so on, in other words, logic, mathematics and the natural sciences. History can be learnt logically, as Collingwood has shown in his beautiful autobiography, i.e. through Archaeology; and so can Geography be learnt by tours and expeditions. In our educational system some provision is made for Mathematics, Logic, Science, etc. but practically none for Archaeology or Geographical tours, and, of course, none whatsoever for crafts. The result is that the outline for the personality of the Youth of 15 to 20 is either not there, or is discernible only through high-powered lenses. Mere information is available. But mostly it is lumber, useless for this rhythmic period and its needs. Insatiable hunger for information is a symptom of growth, if not always of development. Elsewhere, magazines chiefly answer the purpose; here, they do not, or if they do, they work on a combined basis of romance and profit. In such a situation, information knocks at the gate of knowledge, and does not find it. We have a number of young men and women who remain intellectually arrested just at the point where crystallization of the theme could occur but does not. This is really tragic. Only the lucky, and how rare they are, can pass over to the movement of the next rhythm where knowledge takes control. But its pattern is not melodic. It is too full of discordant notes. Such is the character of knowledge that while it seeks to co-ordinate the knower it unsettles him by a battery of alternatives, discriminations and doubts. The knower is both the beneficiary and the victim of knowledge. Our best students in the senior university classes are usually no more than perplexed creatures. Research and post-graduate scholars are more or less integrated, although they pay the costs in terms of indifference to other issues. Naturally, they preserve their self-respect before the defeated urge for fuller development by arguments such as the utter need for specialization in these days of crowded knowledge, rush and efficiency. More of them later. The senior student's case is pathetic. He does not know which books to read. I have passed through that period of confusion, and I can offer a little guidance.

Let us first survey the general position of the important discipline of Economics, a subject with which I have been connected. Economic theory is now busy with three or four important issues: (1) Perfect competition with its model-building of a Static Society and Imperfect competition in the actual order of monopolies of various types. (2) Business-cycles and their mysterious operations. (3) Full employment, and (4) The Optimum in population, business organization, returns, etc. Theories of costs, effective demand, uncertainties and risks, obsolescence, multipliers, sales-curves, marginal revenues are so many refinements of the above. On analysis, they reveal desperate efforts to resolve certain implicit contradictions and explicit conflicts. The former arise mostly from the fact that the classical theories were raised from the phenomena of another age while the present age requires another set of theories to suit its own conditions. On the other hand, the explicit conflicts arise from international economic rivalries. Nations as such are economically organized, but disorder prevails in extra-territorial relations. Autarchy at home and anarchy abroad are inter-locked. To stave off monopolistic competition from outside, to prevent the nation-state from being entangled in the wheels of business-cycles and suffering from the evils of unemployment, to have a number of population that can be supported at a fairly high level of living—these are the problems which every country sets before itself to solve. Economic theories reflect these problems, and try to answer them. It is like lifting yourself by your ears. Now, when you realize the illogicality of the procedure you at once understand that the theoretical attempts cancel one another. Is Full Employment possible in one country when other countries are following their own restrictive policies in pursuit of the same noble objective? How can one country manipulate its optimum population when others hedge in their own numbers by anti-immigration laws? Where is perfect competition when even a retail-trader has some form of monopoly? How can there be any certainty when all conspire to keep up uncertainties? Ultimately, it resolves itself into the ridiculous position that Economic theories are good for my own country and not for yours. In which case, let us stop talking about pure theories, which, if they are pure, are, and must always be, built upon some ultra-national laws of thinking, analysis, and forms of knowledge. Why not then openly declare that Economics have once more become Political Economy, better still Economic Polity? That will be more honest. But honesty or dishonesty is not the issue. The issue is that the knowledge of economic operations and behaviour has entered a crisis in which theories are falling apart by the impact of the stern realities of life. This, however, is no cause of despair to anybody but the intellectual class, to which the youth do not belong, and probably, should not belong. For the youth it is an opportunity for changing tactics. Let them apply the blitz-technique. When the object of knowing is known to be weak, strike hard at the point of weakness, and then roll out like a flood and create pockets of resistance and bases of advance. Only keep your supply-line in tact. The supply-line is your own living-process. The weak-point in economic theories is just where free competition ends and monopoly begins. In so far as the strength of a chain depends on its weakest link, and if there be a desire to break the chain at all, then the selected sphere of study in Economics should be Imperfect Competition and Monopolies. Better still it would be to tackle Monopolies, because the word 'imperfect' suggests a departure from the norm—which, by inference, becomes the 'perfect' and therefore the 'ideal', reducing by a further implication the instances of imperfection to aberrations, and ultimately to a sort of moral vagrancy. Analyse the title of Pigou's *Lapses* from Full Employment and follow his subtle argument. Full Employment is nothing but the ground-assumption of classical Economics, a thing which Adam Smith, Ricardo, and their followers did not discuss *because* it was assumed to be a natural corollary of division of labour that set no limits to production, and therefore, none to employment. That assumption continues to be held by Prof. Pigou and explains the use of the word 'lapse' as the title of his brilliant book.

The situation described above is not peculiar to Economics alone. There are contradictions and crises in Political Science and Philosophy, in History, even in Logic and Metaphysics, in Psychology, and in Science, even in Mathematics. It will be argued, and very legitimately too, that knowledge knows of no other way than that. Yet, the present situation of all forms of discipline is peculiar. Up till now, the intellectual urge for advance came from the desire of pushing back the frontiers of information, inappropriately called knowledge.

Leaving Philosophy aside, the impulse behind knowing was that of bringing the increasing mass of information within a wider scheme and building up a more comprehensive hypothesis. When the mass was unwieldy the usual procedure was the construction of models or nuclei into or around which the marginal fact or information had to be fitted. The difficulty was seldom beyond that of joinery. If the marginal fact was recalcitrant, it was called an exception that only proved the rule, i. e. the model. But in course of time, these exceptions multiplied, and demanded recognition. When they could not be ignored they were given the status of 'special cases'. The trick was to keep in tact the model's peace and equilibrium. But it was soon exposed. Compromises failed when the special cases built up their own models and systems. The new ones were placed in sharp opposition to the old : Capitalism *versus* Socialism, Science *versus* Art, Philosophy *versus* History, Ethics *versus* Jurisprudence, Wave *versus* Quantum, and so on. Framed thus, the true nature of the conflict was not unfolded. The heart of the conflict lay beneath these forms of opposition. What was called the norm and the general rule was reached by an abstracting from a selection of the dominant features of the then prevailing particulars, leaving others in cold storage. These latter belonged to the order of actual, living experience. For example, facts of economic inequality, low wages, unemployment, etc. were matters of life and death for human beings, while the philosophy of Democracy was pushed into the order of theory of Politics. This differentiation was essentially a dichotomization of life into theory and practice. And in so far as the practicalities or the 'realities' were social and theories were the intellectual, individual exercises of a class of people isolated from practice, the nature of the crisis in information lay in the society that wanted to ignore its own differences. Information of the nature of theoretical contradictions, conflicts and crises is the beginning of knowledge; the knowledge of social crisis at the root of modern theories is the essence of the understanding of crises in modern knowledge. Therefore, knowledge of the social crisis is the guiding principle of the selection of books by advanced students who bear the perplexed looks of victims to information. I say, advanced students, because their rhythm has passed from the need of information to fill out their personality to that of understanding in order to render it stable, solid, balanced, and related to other personalities, i. e. to make it socialized. The individual student thus becomes a person.

It is a platitude to say that the movements or rhythms—these words have been used rather synonymously—are not exclusive of each other. The original survives; seldom does the opening movement (the asthayee, or the theme) get lost. It recurs at odd moments; it sometimes envelopes the entire process; in which case, the process becomes monotonous. The second and the third often get telescoped; and the last may as well be a repetition of the first, in which case it is a throw-back. We find it easier to recognize acquaintances growing with recurrence, and we display our pleasure by praise, such as, the character is steady, the personality is rounded, or we theorize by saying that heredity is what counts, education is complete by childhood, that the values of life are universal. Really, it is a job to see, recognize, evaluate an ever-moving movement. And yet it has to be done, if knowledge were to be intimate with reality and a guide to change and be guided by its laws. This job had better be called the sense of history. It is sense, and not information, say about the number of Asoka's wives. It is sense, and not an awareness of the perspective, say about the tavern-life in the London of Queen Elizabeth, Marlowe, Shakespeare or Ben Jonson. It is sense, and not intuition which often goes wrong as it does when reference is made to Rama-Rajya, the Golden Age or the Satya-Yuga. It is sense, because information, awareness and even knowledge are combined here in beautiful proportions. Study of the course of the historical process is essential, but the nature of the study is determined by the object which is the moving pattern. Therefore, through this sense details subserve the whole, and the whole subserves the movement. Sometimes I feel that a study of the historical movement belongs to an order of discipline different from that of records and inscriptions, but I am not sure. Probably, the best training is offered by Logic. At the same time, Logic as we know it does not help the young man to understand the process in which the middle is not always excluded, identity seldom appears, and difference in only an approximation to equality. A study of the Dialectics is indicated. Hegel, however, is too difficult, and ordinary books on Dialectics are hopelessly inadequate. Be that as it may, the sense of history grows with an increase of Dialectical thinking about events in their mass tendencies. Above all, this sense is not a mere aid to contemplation. Detachment there will have to be, otherwise knowledge remains at the mercy of information and information at the mercy of every breeze of emotion that blows. Yet, detachment can be dry and cold-blooded. Those who operate law and order on behalf of 'reasons of State' are supposed to cultivate this desiccated attitude. Doctrinaire Terrorists have often exercised it in the name of discipline. But a graver danger of contemplation or detachment from an Archimedean standpoint arises from its simulacrum, viz. intellectualism. Have you not heard from your intellectual leaders that 'much could be said on both sides of the question?' Capitalism is bad, Protection is good, but both have their points. This kind of pronouncement is all too common in your lecture rooms, and if, young men ask their teachers about their own opinion, they fend you off by all manner of sophistry leaving the world to darkness and to youth. They also strike a pose—the well-known pose of scientific neutrality—they shall not betray their intellect! I am not questioning their intellect, which must be extraordinary. Only, their intellect has not come to much in the way of changing the intellect of India on which a blight has fallen; only their intellect has not helped in making India free, in curbing the depredations of profiteering, of misery and disease. Of course, they could have done all that if their salaries and status were raised either by the Government or by the Capitalists. Meanwhile they will contemplate, yes, contemplate like Pickwick from the top of the stage-coach, or shall I say, like some lunatic on the edge of a leaning, crushing tower of ivory. Whatever else it may be, sense of history is not that luxury. It is wedded to making history, as a Hindu couple are wedded to procreate. Please do not think that I am too hard on my trade union. I am really soft, because I am putting the blame not on the intellectuals as persons but on their non-possession of the sense of history.

So, here's the second principle of book selection. Along with books on science, medicine, engineering, young people should read their authoritative histories. Students read the history of philosophy, of literature, economics, politics, but they are ignorant of the movement of science and technology. Some agitation by the senior students for including the history of these subjects in their courses of study will not be undesirable. If the agitation succeeds a definite social good will ensue. Technicians, when they are handling an instrument or designing it, are under the impression that the potentiality of Science is unlimited. They are not, in fact, they cannot be, conscious either of the crisis on the theoretical side or of the ultimate purpose to which their efforts are bent, viz. profit for the employers. The result is twofold: an extension of the purely mechanical outlook on life into spheres where it does not hold true; and the creation of a certain class slightly superior to the manual labourers, and an attitude that betrays unhealthy symptoms of that feeling of superiority. None of the results would be bad if they corresponded to the actual social process. In that process, the technicians are only respectable employees, white-coated, motor-owning, bungalow-occupying salariat or the managerial body, but employees, none the less. They are not separate from the labourers, but they feel that they are. Hence the danger of technocracy, of 'the managerial revolution' which, if successful, will be a more ruthless type of Fascism with scientific management, rationalization to fortify it. Psychologically, the invasion of the mechanistic attitude is good so far as it carries in its tide the rational way of looking at things. In actual practice, it halts creation, it puts a brake upon revolution, it distorts enjoyment even, by the habit of calculation and accounting of the pros and cons of a critical situation. This calculation of possibilities has often led political fervour astray; it has subtly defended the *status quo* in economic exploitation by the Brahminical subtleties of the

London and the Cambridge schools of Economics; it has reduced the beauty of a poem, a painting, a song into points to be considered'. Just as my main charge against the intellectuals is their inability to make history; so my first plaint against the technicians is that in their pre-occupation with action and operations they bid adieu to their sense of history. The scholastics used to differentiate between making and operation. I wish that the technicians knew this. If they did, they would have realized that the grand evolution of tools into implements, of implements into machinery, of machinery into the gigantic, impersonal monsters that lap surplus with its toothed wheels as primitive gods would lap the blood of its victims –I say, if our technicians knew about it all from their study of the history of science and technology, they could not have remained self-complacent: they would have realized that the changes in the technique were conditioned by some deeper, some more basic changes in the very structure of society. By that knowledge, the technicians would have been humbled; they would have seen through the modern game of crushing them by flattering them; they would have been one with other employees; in short, they would have been socialized. Yes, books on the history of science and technology must be read very seriously. I would say the same thing to the students of medicine. That too was essentially social through its magical rituals, which, as you know, served the whole tribe. Later on, it became curative, as people say. The inwardness of that word is that rich men alone could be cured. Then medicine became preventive, as a result of the awakening of social conscience, which really meant, the *bourgeois* conscience, that unholy concoction of patronizing piety and sneering service. Today, medicine, at least, in one country, is more than preventive; it is constructive. Medicine is now a branch of social engineering, if you care to know the history of medicine. And then what is the position of engineering revealed by its history? The earliest records of civilization are full of magnificent irrigation-schemes and city-buildings. We do not know who made them, but we do know who were the beneficiaries, viz. the people. In the next phase, we come across tombs and pyramids, mausoleums and royal halls exhibiting the splendour of princes and dynasties. Egyptian engineering was bifurcated into the public works relating to the Nile and the private works of individual kings. It is well-known that in this period of the Nile civilization the cementing of the feudal with the religious hierarchy was begun. Civic engineering was continued in Europe and Asia mainly because of the fact that the towns and the cities,—the two anti-feudal elements—had powerful guilds that loved to beautify their cities by their wealth. When the industrial revolution was started, the impulse, the process and the purpose of public works were changed. No longer was engineering civic, because the concentration of factories would not permit it; no longer was the engineering process confined to the operations of slave labour or raw materials, because the work was getting specialized and the materials were slowly being converted into finished materials; no longer was the purpose the same, because the utilization of new power led to a division of the technique into civil, mechanical, electrical, chemical, hydraulic engineering. And the division was dictated by the same reasons, viz. profit by intensification and specialization which had split up the medieval integrity of production. It is not my intention nor is it within my competence to trace the history of engineering.

All that I want to do is to remind the student that the sciences of engineering, the prospects of which appear to be unlimited and unrelated to anything but a few theoretical sciences like Physics and Mathematics, have had their history and that their history shows as much correspondence with the major stages in the evolution of society as for example medicine does. Bearing that in mind, the student of engineering will not fail to understand that the future of engineering lies no longer in the glorification of private individuals or the enhancement of profit of groups of employers, but in public works. Here let me warn you against the usual confusion about the significance of the phrase. Railway-building is also public works; but railway-building for military purposes is not, if it interferes with the natural drainage system, which flushes the fields and renders the countryside healthy. And then, please remember that public works are not meant only to remove unemployment and give jobs to demobilized men and women. Their purpose is to secure planned development and full employment of all the factors of production. A mere study of the engineering courses makes a technician; an understanding of the evolution of engineering transforms him into an engineer capable of discharging his true duties by the society which has entered into a decidedly new phase. It is not a matter of planning *versus* no-planning. It is a question of the social revolution on the answer to which will depend the direction of the development of society, whether it will mark time, look back or go ahead. Planning is vitally connected with social development and its crises, i. e. with the sense of history. A crucial book is Lewis Mumford's *Technics and Civilization*, a volume which I would like to see in every technician's hand.

So far two principles of the selection of books nave been discussed : (1) the crisis in knowledge itself, and (2) the sense of history. They hang together. I want you to attend to this phrase. All disciplines are inter-related. In a certain movement or the rhythm of personal interests, knowledge had better be specialized; but in another, the various movements coalesce and are gathered into a mighty swell. Speaking from the non-personal level, every discipline must needs be special and autonomus by excluding what are called the extraneous elements. But then, a stage comes, as it has come today in every discipline, when the autonomy is broken and the search is made for co-ordination, unity and synthesis. Natural sciences are once more courting natural Philosophy. Political Economy became Pure Economics ; now Pure Economics is wooing Politics and wanting to be Economic Politics which is the meaning of Economics brought out by the Socialists. Therefore, the urge for synthesis of knowledge is the third principle of the selection of books. In the study of humanities, a study of Socialistic literature can save the young student from a lot of beating about the bush. The naming of such books does not come within my purview. But the senior students may as well start with Hogbens' *Maths. for the Million, Science for the Citizen* and Lindsay's *Short History of Culture*. They are first-class attempts at the synthesizing of knowledge, at unfolding its relatednesses to social development.

My discussion has been partial. Only a few principles of book selection have been suggested. I have not enquired into the origins of individual rhythms of the student; probably, they are social by and large. . Nor have I shown the connexion between the individual rhythm and the movement of knowledge, i. e. the history of knowledge It would have been better if I had told you how far the history of knowledge is in the main subordinate to the history of human association. These tasks are left to you. I shall conclude by throwing nother suggestion. There is a rhythm in the life of a nation as in the life of an individual. The analogy should not be ridden to death, and it is better to call it a resemblance and leave it at that. Resemblances, however, may be made to yield a few significances provided they do not minimize the importance of development. With this caution I may proceed to suggest that there are stages in the attainment of a nation's integrity of personality almost equivalent to the child's co-ordination of reflexes and tropism, the shaping of the outline and the filling of it with content, i. e. by expansion, experience and information. Precision of the outline is done by accurate information, learning and scholarship. A nation's learning and scholarship develop like the child's, the adult's and the nature man's. They nucleate around the material needs and are held together by emotions; they spread out with every increase in the horizon of experience; they fix details in accordance with the nation's needs; and when the nation is re-born this accumulated strength of learning and scholarship takes a new leap to render itself worthy of the situation. Then it is Enlightenment, Humanism, Renaissance. Now is the turn of learned men, scholars and clerks, as they are called, to synthesize, to cross-breed so to say, the new Learning with old, experiment with tradition, science with lore, Christian beliefs with Aristotle and Plato, Science with Philosophy, Dialectics with Science and Materialism. In this period Higher Criticism is born. This criticism is no mere textual research, but re-interpretation, or as Neitzsche said, trans-valuation of values Its sole purpose is to show that the departures in the outlook on life are not breaches, but stages in the organic growth Higher Criticism links up the present with the past All prophetic figures have disclaimed originality, all great scholars and critics have preached 'ancient truths' But the Higher Criticism of the Renaissance-periods is bent towards synthesis, towards the fundamental relations between the existing systems of knowledge, and between these and a life of action Such criticism was called 'Critique' in the Europe of the nineteenth century Thus scholarship at times of crisis has by one jump straddled the gulf separating one theory from another, and all theories from action

Is there any doubt that India is passing through a renaissance? If you have none, as I have none, then your attitude towards scholarship and learning should be worthy of the period in which you are fortunately placed Fortunate, because of the simple fact that your individual rhythm is in tune with the national rhythm Therefore, it is your plain duty to study books which are critiques of your knowledge, which give you a synoptic view of the whole system of knowledge, which abolish all barriers that theories erect between one discipline and another Such books are not rare, they have never been rare Revolutionary periods throw them up in plenty Read all such books which have appeared at the crises of history Be inspired by them, do not apply them to your situation as children do. Evaluate them Above all, be encyclopaedic men, men of the Renaissance, specialists in omniscience. Then and only then will you cease to be individuals and become persons, the man in the world of man That is the hope that binds all the principles governing the selection of books.